Mad About God

When We Over-Spiritualize Pain and Turn Tragedy Into A Lesson

By J.S. Park

Cover art by Rob Connelly. http://heyitsrob.com
Interior artwork by Crae Achacoso. http://instagram.com/craaae
http://craelligraphy.com   http://followandreblog.tumblr.com/

All quoted Scripture is from the New International Version 1984, and is also God-breathed and useful for teaching, rebuking, correcting, and training in righteousness.

Citation Information:
J.S. Park, *Mad About God* (Florida: The Way Everlasting Ministry, 2015)

Also the author of:
What The Church Won't Talk About
The Christianese Dating Culture
Cutting It Off

Join me in the journey of faith.

Wordpress. jsparkblog.com
Facebook. facebook.com/pastorjspark
Tumblr. jspark3000.tumblr.com
Podcast. thewayeverlasting.libsyn.com
Twitter. twitter.com/pastorjs3000
YouTube. youtube.com/user/jsparkblog

Dedicated

To my father,
who raised five siblings,
survived two wars,
did not break during torture,
came to America with fifty dollars in his wallet,
and endured a wayward son.

To my mother,
who is the hardest working woman I know,
who slept three hours a night to put me through college,
and taught me that when life is tough,
you can still smile and kick butt.

Mad About The Table of Contents

*"In my deepest wound
I saw your glory,
and it astounded me."*
— St. Augustine, serial sex addict

"We were promised sufferings.
They were part of the program.
We were even told,
'Blessed are they that mourn,'
and I accept it.
I've got nothing that I hadn't bargained for.
Of course it is different
when the thing happens to oneself, not to others,
and in reality, not imagination."[1]
— C.S. Lewis, ex-atheist and grieving widower

---

[1] C.S. Lewis, *A Grief Observed* (NY: HarperCollins, 1961, 1989) p. 48

"Named must your fear be before banish it you can."[2]
— Master Yoda, retired Jedi warrior

[2] *Star Wars V: The Empire Strikes Back*. Dr. Irvin Kershner. Lucasfilm, 1980

I don't have it all figured out and that's okay

[PREFACE 1]

Preface 1
I Don't Have It All Figured Out,
and That's Okay

I don't have it all figured out yet. That's okay.

Well — I'm learning to be okay with it. And that's okay, too.

Like many others, I'm scared of the words, *"I don't know."* If you're a Christian, this is especially vilified in the church. To say, "I don't know" is to admit a weakness in the Bible or to lack confidence in our faith. It's to say, "I brought lighter fluid for my stake-burning." We're afraid to leave some things to mystery because we presume that Christianity must account for every blip and bump in reality. This is most true for tragedy. When life gets hard, the Christian's first reaction is to connect the dots between suffering and faith, and so we have flow charts and flowery prose for *why* this had to happen.

I understand the urge. I hate not knowing. I want to know that my pain isn't going to waste, that God or the universe or this chain of events is somehow leading to a greater good.

But I don't know that.

I don't know that every tunnel has a light at the end. In fact, *trying to fix a diagram on my pain has led to even more pain.* My ego-grip on control over-reaches for an answer, but my fingers constantly slip off the edge of climbing out of the dark. I end up confused about my confusion. I end up interrogating my questions.

The church doesn't deal well with pain. We're taught a God of blessing and promise and reward, and when He doesn't deliver, we can only assume He's abandoned us. Or worse, we attempt to retcon and fan-wank God by filling in for Him. We're told it's "for your growth" and "you're a vehicle for God's glory." This could be true, but it feels like a retrospective cover-up, a hindsight bias. Guys like me who preach on Sundays want to polish our pain with pretty words, because we squirm at the thought of good people losing to evil.

I've done this, too. I've forced one-liners onto my heartache. I've preached a shrink-wrapped theology to the church. I was afraid to say that the tension doesn't always resolve at the end of the thirty minute sitcom.

Yet *that's life*. Plot-holes run amok and plot threads dangle everywhere. We live within an ambiguous, open-ended ending all the time.

I awakened to the slowly growing horror that *it seems God does not always resolve.*

Maybe I'm not supposed to say that. But you've felt it, too. The preacher talks about asking forgiveness from God, but some days, it felt like God owed you the apology.

We've all been mad at something God has done or didn't do — but it's also possible that our ideas about God were driven mad, too. The modern church's prescription for pain didn't work in the mushroom cloud. When you're hurting and the church keeps telling you to read more Bible and pray harder and "just believe," then of course, we'd all go a little mad.

Maybe we were never taught how to get mad with God. Maybe that's why we all went mad about Him.

You could've rejected a version of God that I would reject, too.

Several years ago, a few close friends of mine had betrayed me and I went through a severe depression and anxiety. I ended up taking a two-month sabbatical from ministry. Every time I thought about those who had turned against me, my blood went backwards, but on the surface, I played it cool. I would say the regular Jesus-type things. "God is refining me. This is for my good. I love them anyway." I talked with another friend during my break, and I kept saying things like, "It hurts, but praise God. It stinks, but I trust Him. I'm fine, God's got this." I would start to get mad but then I'd pull back, like dancing at the edge of a cliff. I knew I was stuffing down words, and my friend knew, too.

My friend finally shook his head. "Just stop."

"What do you mean?"

He said five simple words.

"Just say what you feel."

I objected. "Oh, I am. I know God will carry me. It's okay." I almost hissed this out.

My friend said again, "Say what you feel, man. It's me. You don't have to fake it with me."

I opened my mouth to say what a pastor should say: every dime-store Christianese cliché that would look great on Instagram with a selfie. My friend stopped me once more. He said again, "Say what you feel. Just say what you feel. It's me. Don't fake it."

It was our *Good Will Hunting* moment.

I let loose. I let rip a stream of horrible, vulgar, scorching language in a single, sour breath. I wept. I made ugly cry-face. I pounded my fists. My lip even quivered.

It surprised me.

At the end, my friend patted me on the back.

He said, "We all get to do that sometimes."

Of course, I don't recommend this as a normative pattern. I wouldn't do that every day, or that would be a serious problem. But I thought how awful it must be that Christians, most of all, are belittled for showing how we really feel. We contain it under a sugary layer of church-jargon icing because we're scared of the slobbery, vulnerable, pinched-face monster inside, this battered creature that needs to be exposed and set free.

We suppress and repress and regress — but we're scared to express.

I'm imagining God in Heaven, who is probably saying: *Just say what you feel. It's me. You don't have to fake it with me.* Honesty. This is the start of healing.

We all get to do that sometimes.

I hope to make that space here so you can not only say what you feel, but feel what you feel, too.

If you're suffering right now, the last thing you want to do is read about suffering. There's nothing I could say that would alleviate your hurt or solve the *why*. But that's the point. I don't want to close my eyes to the hurt; I will hurt with you as long as it takes.

In our journey together, I don't think we'll find an answer for pain. Many great scholars before me have tried, and I don't think I'll be unlocking that one today. But after great difficulty, maybe we'll arrive at some hard truths: that life is unfair, that the world is selfish, and that many of us will limp to the finish-line. Maybe we'll finally face the dark and no longer repress our wounds. And like life, I won't resolve each chapter with a happy conclusion. I can't do that to you. But I will speak of a certain Truth that I want more than anything to be true.

If you're going through a hard time right now and you need some motivation or inspiration, this probably isn't the book for you. There are many great books for that, but it would be dishonest of me to sugarcoat your coat with more sugar. We're going to dismantle the church culture's simplified take on suffering. We can be honest about how much pain just hurts. I'm going to shake my fist at atrocities, tragedies, evil, and this world gone wrong. If I don't know something, I'll say, "I don't know." I'm going to give you space to vent, rage out, and yell at God. I don't think I can give you tweet-able quotes to highlight or take with you. This will be a grimy, gritty, angry crawl through the mud, gasping for every wisp of air. In the end, I'll tell you about The One who I believe offers healing, but it might not be the pep talk you're looking for.

This book will work much like climbing a jagged mountain. We'll trudge through the valleys and occasionally see glimpses of the summit. We'll make stops and see the steep cliffs for what they really are: long, ugly drops into nothing. Inch by inch, with little light to lead the way, we'll hike by the barest skin of our fingernails. And if you're still with me, we'll attempt a final leap to the peak, where together, we might see all that came before us from the mountaintop. It won't change anything that has happened to us, but perhaps we will each be a little different than when we started, if only to see just another inch.

I have no silver bullet or magical formula to make things better. There's no secret combination of words that will release you from the fog that has stolen you. I wish there was. I'm only asking that you take my hand at the back door of your church to the front door of your heart, between the space of abstract doctrine and your very real hurt, and that before you decide to leave Him behind, you could walk with me through the fog. To wrestle with this over coffee. One plodding step after another. Back to the God that you might not have really rejected, but never found in the first place.

I've been at the bottom, when everyone else has left and I was alone with my hurt in the silence. I've been at the place where I knew all the right theology but none of it reached me.

In this pit, I found a silence even deeper still. It was called honesty, and in that place, He was the only one there. I cried out, and to my surprise, so did He.

— J.S.

PERPETUALLY SKEPTICAL:

Screaming through the Red Sea

Preface 2
Perpetually Skeptical: Screaming Through The Red Sea

I must confess this right up front.

I'm a habitual doubter.

What I mean is, I doubt God all the time.

I came into faith kicking and screaming, or as C.S. Lewis said, *"The most reluctant convert in all of England."*[3] I was an atheist much longer than I've been following Jesus, so my default mode is to doubt. I constantly hunger for empirical, objective evidence to satisfy my roaming mind. The Christian faith has plenty, but it's such a delicate tight-wire to trust within the mystery. For sudden stretches of time, I fall back to the familiar contours of disbelief. I get back to thinking this whole faith-thing is just crazy. Even in the middle of preaching a sermon, I'll get hit with a mind-grenade: *What if this is all for nothing?*

I'm not saying this to appear relatable. I don't wish this kind of skepticism on anyone. It's a constant throbbing splinter in my side and it's downright exhausting.

I've found I'm not alone.

The Big Christian Secret is that *every Christian in history has run into doubts about God.* The doubt that He exists. Even the "best Christians" get lost in the hallway. It's more than just a phase or a season or a dry spell; it's a thick, nauseating fog. There are days I read the Bible and I want to throw it in the trash.

---

[3] C.S. Lewis, *Surprised By Joy* (NY: HarperCollins, 1955) p. 229

I've also found that it doesn't take a doubter like me to doubt Him. I have the misfortune of dealing with it every day: but one day, you'll come to that crossroads, too. When intense pain comes, and it will, you'll be faced with a completely disorienting upheaval of everything you've ever believed. Pain will uppercut your faith in the stomach. And it could make you nauseous.

In suffering, we find out what's really inside. This doesn't mean that God uses suffering to expose our guts. It's not my place to correlate those things. I just want you to be ready for what's coming. I want you to be ready to start over. And I want you to know that doubt doesn't make you a "bad Christian," but an honest one.

You might already be there. We're at the same place. You and I have both wondered what God is doing up there, as He watches our suffering. I wonder why He wouldn't do more. I wonder how He could be good. It's the classic dilemma: *If God is all powerful but He doesn't stop suffering, He must not be good. If God is good but He doesn't stop suffering, He must not be all powerful.*

I don't know how God could be both good and powerful.

It's a question I'll carry until my time on earth is done: and if you're like me, it'll be a lifelong thorn that haunts you every day.

But inversely, **this constant deficit from doubt has prepared me for the bewilderment of pain.** It's like a schoolyard bully that's toughened me up for the boxing ring. I didn't want the bully nor the boxing: but I happened to get both. Please don't think for a second that the bully is a welcome visitor. I also don't mean that God made me a skeptic to be a good sufferer. But if this is how it's going to be, then I'll take the free training. I didn't want this, but it's always in my face — so I have to face it. You will, too.

On one hand, this perpetual skepticism continually throws me off a cliff where I spiral with no bottom and no end. It's torturous. But other days, I'm thankful because it refuses to be filled by temporary fluff. It forces me to land somewhere solid. It has taught me to think through to the bottom of what I really believe. And to even be okay with the unanswered questions.

I'm hoping you'll find a faith that really works. Not perfectly, not always, but enough for both your feet.

When pain hits home and you're walking through that cancer or car accident or earthquake, you want the kind of faith that can face death. In the end, I want a faith that doesn't just tickle my inspiration or give me cute slogans, but a faith that can get beat up by suffering and scholars and satanic evil, and will keep on standing. That only comes when you're able to hold up those doubts to the light, rotate them over and over, and take a second look at every intellectual and existential answer that Christianity has to offer.

True faith, the kind that perseveres through pain and trials and urgency, takes a surgical navigation through all the very difficult questions of life. Only doubts will ever get you to ask them.

I've been learning that doubts do not disqualify me from knowing Him. They're certainly troubling. But sometimes doubt is the persistent prompting to investigate our deepest beliefs, especially when life hits hard. I'm learning that Christianity, if anything, will challenge you to think for yourself. Not *what* to think, but *how*.

The best thing I could tell you is to **question everything, because by questioning everything, you will toss out what doesn't work.** You'll eliminate easy answers that could never sustain the hardest seasons of life.

It's still a fight to find the thing that works. As I tumble, I have to reach for every branch to save me. My grip is weaker than most, but I'm learning perhaps that it's not about the strength of my grip, but the strength of the branch. The amount of my faith matters less than what it holds on to.

I imagine that when Moses split the Red Sea, there were two groups of people.[4]

The first group was composed of victorious triumphant warriors saying, "In your face, Egyptians! This is our God!" They were pumping their fists and thrusting their spears. The second group was composed of doubtful, panicking screamers running full speed through whales and plankton.

I'm a Screamer. I'm a cynic. I'm a critic. I'm a Peter, who can make a good start off the boat, but falls in the water when my eyes wander.

I'm not endorsing a halfway lukewarm faith. I believe God wants us to have a robust, vibrant, thriving relationship with Him. But as for me, I'll be limping to the finish-line. I'm more of a Thomas than a Paul. I'm more Martha than Mary. I'm more David than Daniel.

Yet the Warriors and Screamers all made it through.

---

[4] Inspired by a sermon from Timothy Keller on Exodus 14, called "Getting Out." http://vimeo.com/22669720

It's not easy to have faith the size of a mustard seed. But Jesus promised that this would be enough to move mountains, and I'm learning to be okay with that.

I want to limp with Him to the end.

— **J.S.**

"Lord, I believe; help my unbelief!"
— Mark 9:24

PAIN IS NOT A LESSON:

There isn't a bow-tie

[CHAPTER 1]

Chapter 1

Pain Is Not A Lesson:
There Isn't Always A Bow-Tie

Bow-Ties, Clichés, and Allegories

I don't believe that pain always has a lesson.

I don't believe we can connect the dots on every instance of pain. I can't tell everyone, "God has a plan for your life." I can't always say, "Everything happens for a reason."

A blind theology on suffering only works for the unquestioning. It can work until you have to comfort a young boy with cancer, a mother who lost her son, a suicidal high schooler, a nation oppressed by genocide, a family torn by a school shooting, a violated victim. At this point, it's atrocious to say,

"Pain forces you to grow," or

"It takes a painful situation to change you," or

"God works in mysterious ways."

I think we probably say those things out of good intentions, because it's what we've been taught from Sunday School and the latest bestseller on Overcoming-Your-Valleys. But the longer we live, the more we realize we've been learning isolated clichés that could only work for the suburban quiet of a semi-charmed life. If God is who He says He is, then I don't believe these platitudes are from the heart of God. They can cause even more pain than the original wound.

I want to ask some hard questions. *What if there really is no spiritual lesson from your pain?* What if "God's amazing plan" only makes sense to the privileged and upper-class? What if you never see the reason for why you're going through this horrible ache? What if you're that starving, kidnapped, beat-up kid in a scorched third world country?

If you talk to anyone who's involved in a huge tragedy, every cliché goes out the window. Even citing Bible verses can be tone-deaf and harmful.

I understand the need to allegorize pain into a plotline. All of us, regardless of our beliefs about faith and life and purpose, must construct a narrative in order to make sense out of what happens. We seek to make *sense* and *meaning* out of tragedy, even if it's to only conclude that it's meaningless.

Unfortunately, both secularized Western thought and Christianese clichés have wrought a terrible choke-hold on our understanding of trials and suffering. There are two extremes in both camps that eventually lead to dead-ends, and we get pushed around between them.

In mainstream secular thought, we're taught to either completely **deny** our pain by "positive thinking," or we're taught to **despise** the world because it's cruel, self-centered, and pointless.

Now there's actually a lot of merit to these extremes. To think positive is a great way to find solutions to the world's problems. A good outlook can dramatically benefit your health, your habits, and your marriage. I recommend it to you.

Yet the need to "stay positive" will eventually crush you. The constant clenching to "be-strong" only smothers our real feelings, which leads to collapse. Barbara Ehrenreich, a breast cancer survivor and author of *Bright-Sided: How the Relentless Promotion of Positive Thinking Has Undermined America*, writes about America's obsession with staying positive in hard times. She says in an interview:

> *"What I found was constant exhortations to be positive, to be cheerful, to even embrace the disease as if it were a gift. You know, if that's your idea of a gift, take me off your Christmas list ... But it went along with the idea that you would not get better unless you mobilized all these positive thoughts all the time ...*
>
> *"But, you know, imagine the burden that is on somebody who's already suffering from a very serious disease, and then, in addition, they have to worry about constantly working on their mood, you know, like a second illness ... I can't tell you how many times I have read people who have lost their jobs in this recession in the newspaper saying, 'But I'm trying so hard to be positive.' Well, maybe there's no reason to be positive. Maybe you should be angry, you know? I mean, there is a place for that in the world."[5]*

It's also true that this world can be a harsh place that requires us to dispel our naïve illusions. It's healthy to have a realistic assessment of the world and to prepare for all the eventualities of life.

But in the long run, cynicism can become unsustainable. An overly negative view of the world is toxic and draining. Viktor Frankl, a Holocaust survivor, was in Auschwitz, which was

---

[5] http://www.democracynow.org/2009/10/13/author_barbara_ehrenreich_on_bright_sided

perhaps the worst concentration camp during WWII.[6] He writes in *Man's Search For Meaning* about several types of prisoners. The first kind lost hope very quickly, resulting in illness, lethargy, or an expedited death. The second kind kept hope during their imprisonment, but upon release at the end of the war, their desired hope for freedom didn't match their expectations, and they grew disillusioned and bitter. Yet a third kind of prisoner was able to transcend both their imprisonment and the unmet expectation of freedom, so that neither hell nor hype would control them.[7] Their survival was based on neither a too positive or too negative view of life. Cynicism is sometimes necessary, but it can be a prison even when the pain is over.

The Christian faith also contains these two extremes: either smiling through suffering or looking to Heaven. One denies and the other despises.

Again, there's some merit to both sides of the spectrum. But taken to their end conclusions, Christians tend to gloss over tragedy by enforcing an all-too-convenient narrative for all of life's woes. There's a secret fear that if we cannot explain tragedy, then we're somehow insulting the all-knowing God. This is considered "putting words in God's mouth."

Many Christians also tend to relegate suffering to a footnote as we look to Heaven, so we end up despising the world — but this diminishes the pain of people hurting *right now*. Some of the early church grew so obsessed with Jesus coming back, they quit

---

[6] Just a note that I'm aware of violating Godwin's law in order to make a point. Godwin's law is when the topic of "Hitler" or "Nazis" is brought up as a point of extreme argument, which instantly means the argument has lost. However, I found Frankl's observations such an insightful piece of history that I relay it here as a fascinating, painful look into human nature.
[7] This is a highly simplified account of Viktor Frankl's memoirs, which deserves careful reading for its nuanced and uneasy look at evil, suffering, and hope.

their jobs and watched for every sign of the Apocalypse. Apostle Paul, who wrote half the New Testament, had to write two entire letters to the church in Thessalonica rebuking their laziness. Even Paul knew that the concepts of Heaven and the "Second Coming" were not consolation prizes. We are here, in the dirt, and we need better than settling up.

—

I believe that sometimes, pain is just pain.

Sometimes it just hurts.

Until we see the face of God, we mostly won't know the *why*. Even then, I'm not sure there will be a neat bow-tie at the end.

In the waiting, I don't want to moralize my pain. I refuse to connect the dots at someone who is hurting in the lowest bottom of their soul. I cannot pretty-up grief with retrospective hindsight or poetic reflection. I will not diminish someone's tragedy into an allegory. I cannot take a human wound and flip it into a cute outline for my logical sensibilities.

Pain sucks. It's dirty. It's not fit for books and movies. It doesn't always resolve. It's not romantic. It doesn't need an answer or a fix-it-all. That drives me crazy, but nearly every answer has always come up short and trite and impractical. Pain is a terrible teacher who we try to force answers from, but maybe we're demanding something that it can't give.

I want to let pain be as it is, because it's part of what makes us human. It's to be experienced, not always explained. I'm trying to be okay with that. I'm trying to live with the wounds. I want to let life unfold, not to escape or avoid or deny, but to let the deepest hurt become part of me, a part of our human story.

Certainly there is some accommodating theology (which we'll talk about in these pages), but I think we jump to that too quickly. The hard truth is that we live on a fractured planet with a broken people who are dislocated from their source. Ugliness is bound to happen, and when we try to moralize or spiritualize, we find ourselves on unsteady ground with unanswered longing.

The Non-Theology Theology: The Fear of Being Irrelevant When Bad Things Happen

Here's the other problem.

We overreacted to bad theology with more bad theology.

A new wave of Christians are angry about the simplistic clichés for suffering. Now it's en vogue to say, *"Just be there for someone."* No talk, but only presence. *"Relational, not propositional."* This is the new casual Christian, laid back about doctrine and suspicious of scholars — or else you're a jerk.

I understand this. It's insensitive to preach cold, abstract theology at hurting people. I absolutely believe relational presence is a primary element of Christian faith. Those scholars who explain pain: we throw them under the Religious Nut Bus. We use clever counter-cultural terms like "theological bullsh_t meter"[8] because self-aware irony makes us more acceptable.

But really, I wonder how much of this is just a fear of backlash. I wonder how much of our talk on "relational

---

[8] http://www.patheos.com/blogs/nakedpastor/2013/04/the-meaning-of-suffering-and-theological-bs/

intimacy" is really just people-pleasing, just more b.s. to cover for our cowardice.

It seems we want to be "relational" only to appear more relevant. We're scared of having the unpopular opinion.

Are we really that afraid to discover a robust, vibrant, encouraging, lucid theology on God during our struggles? Are we really that desperate to cater to the modern skeptic with a watered-down version of pseudo-Christian humanism?

Because if there really is a good, powerful, all-knowing God, then I want to know about Him. If He's real, He has to be the *only one* who can actually do work on our hearts in the heartache. This means eventually, not too soon and not too late, we need to find all of Him.

At some point, there must be something offered more than our silent presence. There must be a worldview that accommodates for atrocities and tragedies. We must have a hope that is both *displayed in actions* and *spoken with words.* Our comfort means nothing if it's merely comfort for its own sake.

If our world is really this fractured, then it appears the Christian faith can offer the *best thing possible.* It offers both the *pathos* and the *logos,* both a presence and a reason. I can't stay silent about that.

Even if my voice shakes and it sounds crazy out of my mouth and even if you reject me, the least I can do is tell you about it. I can tell you about The One who saved me and changed me and is with me through everything that has ever happened.

I believe this is all going somewhere. The Christian faith says we're in a story with a direction. We don't always know the *why,* we don't always know what God is really doing, we don't always find it easy to trust Him.

But I want to get there. Not with shortcuts or shoddy scaffolding, but really wrestling with the truth to the end.

Within this uneasy tension between a hostile, broken world and a perfectly loving God, we can't settle for formulas. We can't go for flow charts and diagrams. When we attempt to make bullet-points of our pain, we do deep harm to our view of God and life. We expect God to owe us, or worse, that He hates us. But we don't have to be imprisoned by such a shallow view of Him. We can build something better, because He offers something deeper.

It's here that I don't expect every pain to wrap up neatly. I wouldn't dare to tie up all the dangling threads. Instead, I look for the strength and resources to help me endure suffering when it comes. It's coming. I don't look to make sense of the pain, but a way forward through the scars.

This means letting go of the lies I have believed from both our secular philosophies and simplistic Christian doctrines. Maybe it's too strong to call them "lies," but rather, they're unwieldy place-holders that we forced into the gaps, and they only betrayed us. Underneath the layers we've added, I believe there's a true peace that transcends us and transforms us, that doesn't keep the hurt from hurting, but keeps me moving despite myself.

Here, we find the presence we need and the reason to keep going. We can dismantle some of the lies we believe.

Then, we'll find something greater for our belief.

"There is a time for everything,
and a season for every activity under heaven:
a time to be born and a time to die,
a time to plant and a time to uproot,
a time to kill and a time to heal,
a time to tear down and a time to build,
a time to weep and a time to laugh,
a time to mourn and a time to dance,
a time to scatter stones and a time to gather them,
a time to embrace and a time to refrain,
a time to search and a time to give up,
a time to keep and a time to throw away,
a time to tear and a time to mend,
a time to be silent and a time to speak,
a time to love and a time to hate,
a time for war and a time for peace."

— Ecclesiastes 3:1-8

IT'S ALWAYS TOO SOON:

A time of mourning before the morning

[CHAPTER 2]

Chapter 2
It's Always Too Soon:
A Time of Mourning
Before The Morning

Say It All or Say Nothing

I'm friends with a married couple whose child suffered a severe head trauma as a baby from a faultless car accident. Their son will never be able to walk and talk like other children and he'll most likely need assistance for the rest of his life. The rest of their extended family is still finding out.

Within the first six months of the accident, I came over to be with them. The mother was especially distraught. Both of them had completely stopped attending church. I felt like my job as a pastor was to cheer them up, encourage them onward, and maybe even get them back to church again. They were both once heavily involved; we had once thought about planting a church together; the father was the first person who introduced me to C.S. Lewis. They didn't exactly hate God now, but faith had been oozing out from them like blood loss, rendering them far from God by slow, imperceptible degrees.

We sat together in front of their fireplace, their home adorned with medical equipment and various beeping machines. Their child was fitted with a customized head-piece because he just had brain surgery.

At one point, I said, "I believe everything happens for a reason."

The mother turned and said, "I don't believe that."

I didn't expect this response. "No ...?"

She said, "Fine. Tell me exactly what reason."

I tried to answer both her and her husband, "Maybe we won't find out in this lifetime, but we'll find out when we get to God." I thought this was the smart thing to say.

She replied, "How does that help me right now?" I paused. She said, "And what if there's no reason?"

In my seminary-trained brain, I couldn't fathom the possibility.

I said, "Maybe the reason is to help other people who are going through the same thing."

She said just as quickly, "What people? How would I help them? What do we talk about? I tell them what you told me? I can help people without going through this. Tell me exactly how I would help other people who are going through the same thing."

I should've let it go here, but I couldn't. I said, almost in a whisper, "Maybe we can choose to use it for good."

She said, "That has nothing to do with anything I just said. You said there's a reason and you can't tell me why. You said I can help people but I can do that anyway. You said I can use it for good but that means I have to do the work instead of God. I don't want to exploit my son into a sensational inspiration. I can't find any possible explanation that would make sense for this to happen to her no matter how great it sounds when I 'get to God,' because nothing could ever take back the hell we're going through. Even if that happened, that would mean any 'lesson' we learned from all this would be pointless if God is just going to wipe it away. So no, I don't believe this happened for a reason. I will never believe it. Some things just happen."

I could tell she hadn't planned this. I had provoked a raw nerve in her with my vacuum-sealed platitudes.

It was silent for a while. Then I said, "You're right." I coughed, a little too loud in my ears. "I don't know. I don't know any reason this could've happened or any reason that would ever explain this to you. Or me."

Her husband said two words.

"Finally. Honesty."

At A Loss of Words For a Loss of Words

When a friend is going through a hard time:

What exactly can we say?

The first type of response that usually comes to mind is, *"It'll be okay. You'll be all right. Things will work out. It won't last forever."*

This could be called a **Reassurance**. It's a good thing and we could always use reassuring. If anything, it fills the silence.

The second type is, *"Look on the bright side. Keep your head up. Eyes on the prize."*

This could be called **Advice** or **Wisdom**. It has a practical function that's supposed to motivate you to feel better. It can be helpful to move past what's happening.

The third type is, *"Everything happens for a reason. It's for the best. This is meant to be."*

This is a much deeper response and implicitly assumes an external plan outside us. It could be called a **Framework** or

Philosophy. It's often the most necessary thing to survive in the long-term, because we need a mental apparatus to put the pieces back together.

The bad news is: *All these responses eventually fall apart at the seams*. The even worse news is: *The deeper you explain your pain, the more it can disappoint you*.

The first one, *Reassurance*, is the fastest to go but the easiest to let go, too. The second one, *Advice*, might keep us going a little longer, but the weight of maintaining advice will always crush us. The last one, the *Framework,* is what we most invest in, but when it crumbles, we're wounded at the most profound level. Very often, we're more hurt than the original wound. It's the difference between losing a wallet and losing a house.

The more you expect something to hold you up, the more it can let you down.

When a Framework is theological in nature, or when the Philosophy becomes a *Theology,* this hurts the worst. Christians invest into a kind of faith that inadvertently says, "Good people are rewarded and bad people are punished" or "God works all things for our best." When this doesn't pan out, we write off God as a callous, selective, distant prankster who never cared about us anyway. Other Christians might blindly force a smile and keep saying, "One day we'll know," through clenched teeth while it grinds away at our sanity.

This is why I understand the jaded prodigal. He couldn't reconcile the pain of this world with a God who claims to be good. I know why we cringe when the preacher talks about suffering, because he's describing the desert from his lawn chair in a palace.

I understand those seeds in Jesus's parable that began to grow but were choked out by trouble and persecution. Maybe they weren't sell-outs, but no one offered them a framework to build their house on stable ground. I don't think anyone *tries* to have an incomplete theology on pain. We're given small reassurances and scraps of advice and a quick philosophy, but the clouds come and we're left naked in a snowstorm shaking our fist at a godless sky.

I understand my two friends, the married couple, because though they were making the best of a tough situation, it didn't help them to force another framework that had failed them. I would only be adding more pain to their pain.

Who's Learning The Lesson?

The most popular framework in church is that God specifically assigns a trial to discipline you. In other words, "God is putting me through a trial to refine me."

The three most popular passages for this are James 1:2-5, Hebrews 12:5-13, and 1 Peter 4:12-13. I won't reprint them here, but if you decide to read them, please read the surrounding chapters, too.

The one problematic conclusion is that none of these passages are about learning from pain. These verses only speak to *persecuted Christians who were suffering for their faith*. God was encouraging them to hang on. The original writers of these verses were speaking to a specific group of people under the dictatorship of a Christian-hating nation.

I do believe, of course, that these passages are saying God cares about us. I believe they reflect the heart of God, for both persecuted believers and hurting people. But I can't conclude in good conscience that "God puts us through trials for our good." A God who throws us into a refining fire is nothing more than a sadistic demigod who holds us by puppet strings.

You don't have to agree with me. I don't for a second think I've "unlocked" the secret meaning to these passages. If I'm wrong, I want to know. I only want us to investigate thoroughly, and in doing so, dispel some myths that have been hurting us all along. My worry is that you'll arrive at a tailor-made theology which will come up short and leave you sour. I don't want that for you. And I believe, neither does God.

Two Hours Too Soon

For a while, I chalked up that whole conversation with my married friends to a miscalculation of timing. It was *Too Soon*. I had spoken too early in their ordeal. Maybe with a proper lapse of time, they'd be ready to reclaim their faith.

I have another friend who recently failed a major test to move up in his career. He opened the envelope with the scores in front of his wife, and she saw him twist up into a defeated mess.

My friend told me, "She tried to cheer me up. Right on the spot. Like she kept rubbing my shoulder and saying mean things about the testing people. But man, it made everything worse somehow. I know she was doing the right thing in her mind, but I just didn't want that. Not right then. Not ever. I told her, *'Just give me two hours.'"*

He locked himself in a room for a couple hours just mad at himself. He had missed the passing score by one point.

I asked, "How are you feeling now?"

"I'm okay and I'm not okay. I have to retake it. For one point."

I'm okay and I'm not okay.

I started thinking about this tricky idea of timing.

I started to think that *Too Soon* is perhaps *always* true. If you fail a big test or your child is disabled or there's cancer or a car accident, these are clouds that hang over us for the rest of our lives. We can get over them, but they become a part of us that's permanently woven into our history. We'll always feel them, like the fault line of a broken bone on a rainy day. I had trouble imagining an appropriate time when we could each say with finality, "It's okay." I started thinking that we live within this tension of, *"I'm okay and I'm not okay,"* and it would be inhuman to rush us through the mourning process. Even insulting.

I've had dozens of conversations like this, where it wasn't just 'Too soon," but it was *Never Enough.* It wasn't about timing, but wholeness. It could be two minutes or two hours or two dozen years — none of my little clichés were holding up. The reassurances and advice and philosophies *never* worked, no matter when I said them. I wasn't even sure they were looking for something to *work*, and in all my moments of wreckage, I wasn't looking for that either.

Everyone was telling them "It's going to be okay" — but sometimes this isn't true. Lifelong illness gets worse. A failed test or a rejection letter can break the course of your life. The death of a loved one is a permanent splinter in your heart. What I kept finding is that not all these things would completely shake the faith out of someone, but it turned "faith" into an extra burden that made the person *worse* and not better.

The end result of these frameworks kept blowing up in my face. If *everything happens for a reason,* that means all of life is prepackaged and predestined without me. I can sit back while trials unfold and I become a passive participant in all that happens. I wouldn't pursue justice for my fellow suffering friend, because it's all "part of God's plan." It's a blanket answer that instantly shuts down dialogue.

When I filtered trials into teachable moments, I kept forgetting that *I don't have the right to rush your healing.* I don't have the right to tell you what your pain might be teaching you, if there's anything to be taught at all.

We hardly have room to mourn anymore. When you have an entire Sunday service full of jumping and singing and hollering and flashy preaching, then the church is the least appropriate place for the grieving person. It wasn't that my friends wanted to stay sad and somber all the time. It was that the gap between *mourning* and the *morning* had no room. It was shut too quickly. At church, we're mostly expected to maintain a fervent rock-star emotionalism that tops the last week, every week, until we're eating Scripture and puking praise. It's why our trials hit us so hard: because we're given small crumbs of idealism to pull us out of reality. It tears us in half. We're often taught to strive above our situation to a higher place, as if I could flip a switch and jump to the front row. I was never told about the writhing limbo between *okay* and *not okay.*

In our pain, we've forgotten how to grieve.

Verses Not Fit for Coffee Cups and Wallpaper

Of course, I don't think the solution is to stay enraged forever. Eventually, there has to be a way to process all this grief — that on one hand, allows us to feel, but on the other hand, does not let the feelings decide who we are. There must be a way to ride the limbo.

I want to suggest to you, dear friend, a tough idea.

Dishonesty with yourself will kill you — but directionless rage will kill you, too.

We need honesty with a direction. In other words, we need a safe haven that will heal us and a sacred base that will guide us.

To smother the heartbeat of what you're going through will choke out your humanity. But to give in to all you're feeling might choke you out, as well.

I believe the Bible offers space for all our rage, and at the same time, a direction that doesn't end in total implosion. The Bible actually has very little trouble with this. There's a sort of naked honesty all over the place. In this, we also find the bare makings of a framework that could work.

In Scripture, there are two categories of honesty, one called *Imprecatory Prayers* and the other called *Lamentations.*

Imprecatory Prayers are throughout David's Psalms and the Book of Habakkuk, in which the writers call down ruinous curses upon their enemies. This isn't like "the enemy" in a triumphalist self-affirming theology when we're talking about that girl at work or the pastor down the street. This is about real *enemies* who were invading Israel to pillage and ransack their homes. David and Habakkuk and others were angry at God and angry at the invading soldiers. When you read the three chapters of the Book of Nahum, it sounds like one big middle finger to the country of Nineveh. It borders on racism and genocidal mania. At one point Nahum says he wants to throw his feces at the Ninevites in battle.[9] While the Old Testament is often accused of gratuitous bloodlust, I can at least understand men like David and Habbakuk and Nahum. If my home and my nation was being displaced by armed terrorists and they were setting fire to the local grocery store and beating up my dog, I would probably call curses on them, too. It puts the Old Testament in an entirely different light when I know the injustice they were dealt, especially lines like, *"Happy is the one who seizes your infants and dashes them against the rocks."* It's not okay, but it's how they felt.

Lamentations, or lamenting, is a slobbery kind of agony found in Psalms, Jeremiah, Isaiah, and of course, Lamentations. While imprecatory prayers cry out against the oppressor, lamentations often cry out against God, or even ourselves.

Most of us skip these verses for plaques and t-shirts and we pick the perky ones. There's been a glut of Christian blogs that have pictures of a sunset over an ocean with a Bible verse or a quick one-liner, and most of them are viral. To be truthful, I'm not against this, because I have a similar blog. We do need quick pick-me-ups and there's nothing wrong with that, at all. I don't mean to bash anyone with an inspirational blog, because you're doing a good thing.

---

[9] This section on Nahum is inspired by artist Jim LePage, which you can find here: http://jimlepage.com/blog/word-nahum
The verse in question is Nahum 3:6.

Such blogs make the impression that the Bible is a collection of daily motivation: but you'll be disappointed when you actually read through it. It gets dark, fast.

The Bible is chock full of unresolved outrage that doesn't fit coffee cups and bumper stickers, instead swelling with the stench of festering wounds. For all our fascination with feel-bad movies and gloomy art, none of it comes close to the darkest valley of the Bible.

You won't see these on your blog wallpaper:

How long, O LORD? Will you forget me forever?
 How long will you hide your face from me?
How long must I wrestle with my thoughts
and day after day have sorrow in my heart?
How long will my enemy triumph over me?
— Psalm 13:1-2

I have seen all the things that are done under the sun;
all of them are meaningless, a chasing after the wind.
— Ecclesiastes 1:14

Their infants will be dashed to pieces before their eyes;
their houses will be looted and their wives violated.
— Isaiah 13:16

I am the man who has seen affliction by the rod of the LORD's wrath.
Even when I call out or cry for help, he shuts out my prayer.
He has broken my teeth with gravel; he has trampled me in the dust.
— Lamentations 3:1, 8, 16

How long, O LORD, must I call for help, but you do not listen?
Or cry out to you, "Violence!" but you do not save?
Why do you make me look at injustice? Why do you tolerate wrongdoing?

Destruction and violence are before me; there is strife, and conflict abounds.
Therefore the law is paralyzed, and justice never prevails.
The wicked hem in the righteous, so that justice is perverted
— Habakkuk 1:2-4

"It is more bitter for me than for you,
because the LORD's hand has turned against me!"
— Ruth 1:13, spoken by Naomi

"Lord," Martha said to Jesus,
"if you had been here, my brother would not have died."
— John 11:21

And perhaps the most infamous of all:

Jesus cried out in a loud voice, "Eli, Eli, lema sabachthani?"
(which means "My God, my God, why have you forsaken me?")
— Matthew 27:46

These are troubling: most of all Jesus's cry of dereliction on the cross.

Many of these resolve; many of them do not.

It's like a song in the key of G that ends on a C chord. We're left hanging. There's a suspended uncertainty. It makes us nervous, and we don't want to talk about it.

But here's why I'm hopeful.

If the men and women of the Bible like David, Solomon, Isaiah, Jeremiah, Habakkuk, Naomi, Martha, and Jesus did not water down their hurt, *then we don't have to, either.*

The Bible is not a glossy, photoshopped, picture-perfect album of crisp, clean, white-teeth people. They doubted. They were mad at God. They were mad at each other. They questioned *why*.

Before we get to a place of resolution, I believe God wants openness. Between us and Him, and between each other. The freedom to be freely you and me. That's nothing you haven't heard before: but it's so incredibly difficult to muster. To not just be open about what happened to us, but to be open about what's happening *in* us.

If you've been beating yourself up for the way you feel — that's an unfair pressure on yourself that I don't think God wants for you. *You don't owe anyone a better version of yourself through your pain. You're allowed to openly wrestle and to simmer in the unanswered questions of your suffering.*

Maybe God has been saying all along, *This is where you can say everything.*

On the other hand, some of us have been angry for so long that we haven't reached for the help we need. We've stayed static. In each Bible passage where someone was lamenting, they were scrambling to stay above the water. Their pain had a momentum. *By being mad at God, they were acknowledging God.* They were looking for how to stand on their feet again, even if that meant scraping up the side of a dirty wall for a long, long time. Inversely, and maybe ironically, the more you know your own hurt, the more desperately you can seek the strength for the next step. If I'm going to be mad, I want to yell at the heavens, where there's healing.

My married friends were allowed to doubt, to seethe, to wonder.

My friend was allowed to have his two hours, and longer.

Dear friend, you're allowed to grieve, too.

You can be free of easy answers.

You are free to tell Him that it hurts.

The important thing is,

*I would much rather be mad **with** God than mad without Him.*

There's an unabashed rawness in Scripture in which no one held back on telling God how they felt, while they also told God how they felt about Him. It was the only way they could be both honest and whole.

Your feelings are not wrong. Your hurt is not wrong. We don't have to feel bad about feeling bad. It's within this space of truly confronting our pain that those encouraging verses actually make sense. It's only when we know the bottom do we begin to see what's above us.

I hope we're not afraid of this in our conversations over coffee, where we let the pain sting for a while. I hope we're not too shy for a candid breakdown. I hope you know that your venting and frustration and anger are welcome here at this table. I also hope our honesty is not just for honesty's sake, but can be wrestled with in the very anger we're swimming in, to the very end.

As Pastor Matt Chandler has said, and perhaps many have said before him:

"It's okay to not be okay. But it's not okay to stay there."

I'd like to suggest that it might be okay to stay there, even for a while.

I feel things deeply. I don't know how else to feel them.
I cry reading the news.
I laugh reading text messages. I get inspired by underdogs.
I get angry for you more than you're angry for yourself.
It doesn't mean I'm crazy.
It just means I'm okay with being me.
If you're not okay with that,
I'm okay with you not being okay with that,
but it still won't change how I feel things.

— J.S.

THE RIGHT KIND OF SAD STORY:

Inspirational sales pitch and sexy cancer

[CHAPTER 3]

Chapter 3
The Right Kind of Sad Story: Inspirational Sales Pitch and Sexy Cancer

The Mass Capitalization of Suffering

In the battle to be honest about our hurt, I want to protect you from a bizarre subculture that has made it impossible to get truly honest.

I'm talking about the **Romanticism of Pain.**

The end result of this fascination with pain gets us to some weird, damaging places.

Jessica Tidwell, a missionary, explains in a blog post how she expected Nairobi to be impoverished and ruined and "for kids that were half naked and covered in bug bites."[10] Instead, it turned out to be more or less like a typical American city, with malls and grocery stores and skyscrapers. She writes, "John [my husband] could tell I was discouraged. That my heart wasn't 'in' today." She was "comforted" by another missionary couple who assured the rest of Kenya was not as affluent as Nairobi.

I can't judge Jessica. Really. I don't think she had wrong motives and she's grateful that it wasn't as bad as she expected.

---

[10] https://jestidwell.wordpress.com/2015/02/02/it-didnt-happen-like-i-thought-it-would/

But this is also a systemic issue in the church. Most mission trips are just glamorous photo tours. It's what one blogger calls "Poverty Porn." We want to be the savior of Africa. I want to be the knight in someone else's misery.

This mentality has led to some false, harmful ideas.

Myth 1 — Your suffering can inspire your way out of suffering.

There's a very lively Subculture of Suffering which presumes that pain can be used for *motivation* towards a better life. For the Christian, we assume that God Himself must be using pain to motivate us.

I don't think the intentions are bad here. We all want something good to come out of something bad. This is totally understandable, because again, we scramble to make sense out of the senseless. But when everyone is using everyone else's pain to motivate them, including their own, it de-personalizes the pain. It marginalizes the actual hurt into a mechanical apparatus, which often leaves the hurting person behind.

It's also exhausting. Someone once told me, *"When you see where you are and where you want to be, let that distance inspire you."*

That's a nice notion, really. It's worked a couple times at the gym.

But in the space between a busted up world and a perfect idealism, that sort of distance only drains me. While there are many great inspirational stories of rags-to-riches and overcoming disabilities, I get weary of hearing that pain is a "blessing in disguise." Most days, it's frustrating and infuriating. To say, "Rise above your surroundings" only diminishes the hurt of poverty and abuse. To call disability a "gift" skips the long, lonely nights of self-loathing and fear.

This sort of self-help assumes that you even have the most basic comfort and resources to do something about it. Most of us don't have the privilege or access to rise up out of our situations. Not everyone can fight upward by sheer willpower. It's only adding one more burden to the burden.

Myth 2 — Suffering is graded on a scale of social acceptability.

You've seen this happen. We dress up suffering and make it sexy. Marketable Pain.

What I mean is, we think pain is inspiring as long as it meets our Hollywood sensibilities of pain. At some point, we turn a blind eye on un-marketable agony. Nearly every movie portraying someone with a disability shows a hidden talent, like *Rain Man* or *Forrest Gump* or *A Beautiful Mind.* You won't see a movie hero who regularly loses control of his bowels or is hideously scarred from head to toe.

It seems we only like the right kind of sad stories. Especially the ones framed for charity. I don't mean to be glib. I just think it's hard to make an appealing fundraiser for Tourette syndrome, or constant incontinence, or no limbs, or a face scarred by third degree burns. Donations are higher when you're shown a picture of one starving girl than when you're told that millions are dying.[11] The media will jump on the polished sort of pain that makes for a sentimental news story.

---

[11] http://www.npr.org/blogs/goatsandsoda/2014/11/05/361433850/why-your-brain-wants-to-help-one-child-in-need-but-not-millions

We demand sexy cancer. We romanticize the highlights and forget the rest. Dr. Robert A. Clark, in an interview about cancer portrayed in Hollywood, says,

> *"Cancer can involve a lot of messy things — surgeries with colostomies and urinary bags and some kind of nasty things. That's not something that filmmakers typically want to portray. It's probably also a little more emotionally compelling when you have a 30-year-old victim instead of a 75- or 80-year-old victim."*[12]

If you've ever been around a colostomy bag or have given a partial bed-bath or dealt with oozing sores: none of this is shown in the chick flicks when the young attractive guy visits his sick lover in the hospital. The woman gets prettier as the disease spreads.

We each have a secret number scale that grades value based on attractiveness. I've served at a homeless ministry now for over four years, and when I bring friends along, most of them come with me once or twice and then never bring it up again. I don't believe the homeless ministry is a calling for everyone. But I notice that my friends who stop going had an idea of what it would be like, and it's quickly shattered when they see the emotionally unstable, the ones who haven't showered in weeks, the misery and muttering and bloodshot eyes. They expected that moment in a movie when there's a special connection and someone sings "Ain't No Mountain High Enough," but life isn't like that. Suffering isn't like that. Not even close.

---

[12] http://www.huffingtonpost.com/2013/02/25/cancer-in-movies_n_2758417.html

It doesn't make me better than anyone. It means that no one told them how hard it would be. Our expectations distort our efforts.

Myth 3 — Suffering brings us closer together.

Some of us even *desire suffering,* because it helps us appreciate life. There's some truth to this. Traumatic events have a way of bringing us closer. A loss will cut through the petty concerns of less important matters. Nothing brings more crystal clarity than a relative in a hospital bed.

But after it brings us together, there's a grueling endurance that goes beyond the moment of tragedy. Most of us only have a pretty picture of pain in our heads, so we're not prepared for the aftermath. If you're the hurting person, you know what I mean. You've been abandoned by friends who checked out early because they couldn't handle your smell. When your pain crossed a threshold, they left.

Suffering can certainly bring us together, but it's not an automatic reflex. There are some stories of pain that are so difficult that no one wants to get involved — so we ignore an entire class of "irredeemable" people. It's impossible to romanticize the everyday strain of caring for a permanently ill family member. There are no montages full of high fives and head nods. A hyper-romantic view of pain leaves out the troubled and traumatized. No one wants the orphan with schizophrenia and multiple sclerosis. At some point, we leave behind the difficult cases. We can't stand the smell.

Pain is never, ever sexy: and I want to prepare you for the long haul. The only way forward is to confront the ugliness inside and out.

Pain-Sensationalism:
Trophies and Epiphanies

I bring this up for two reasons.

The first reason is that using someone's painful story as a motivation only dehumanizes the actual person in the story. It steals their hurt to make it about *me* instead of them. It makes your hurt into my own personal catharsis.

I don't mean that we quit sharing our hurt together. I mean that hearing about your hurt must inspire me to move toward *you*, not toward me.

Imagine you tell me that you were robbed or cheated or you lost your job, and in that moment, I say, "Your suffering really inspires me." Your pain isn't up for grabs this way.

We see this in movies all the time. The protagonist is a total slacker until he meets the disabled kid or the girl with cancer, and suddenly he's moved to action and compassion. *The actual suffering people are only used as secondary props to fulfill the hero's savior-narrative.* And that's only if their suffering is attractive and whimsical.

You might have shared a personal heartbreak with your pastor, only for the next Sunday to have your pastor preach it in the pulpit. Maybe he had your permission, but it still felt cheap and tacky. I have to apologize here because I've done this, too: I've turned someone's very real hurt into a rousing allegory.

This is the opposite of a Cautionary Tale, which is a manipulative scare tactic to guilt-trip you into doing the right thing. Instead, it's a Positive Survivor Tale, which can be very moving, but can become so impersonalized that we lose sight of the actual person in the story. I'm not comfortable with turning someone's tragedy into a trophy for self-improvement. I'm not okay with using such suffering to conclude, "It could always be worse," as if I should be thankful that it happened to someone else. These stories are about real people who really suffered and are probably still suffering.

Again: *Your hurt ought to inspire me to move toward you, not me.*

The second reason is that we often feel shamed or discouraged if our pain doesn't have an "upward mobility." We're taught that our tragedies must be met with maturity and midnight epiphanies, or else you're "wasting your pain." It's as if your pain only counts if you come out on top at the end. It would be really great if you did come out on top, but no one talks about the terrible road to get there.

Of course, I'm encouraged to see others rise from their ashes. The problem isn't the actual victory. It's when we perceive these happy endings to be a template for our own lives and we get frustrated that we can't catch up to this invisible standard. We paint an inaccurate picture of a "beautiful struggle" when struggling in real life is often graphic and gross.

Trying To Witness Versus How You Really Are

I know that a lot of this is the church's fault. It's *my* fault.

I don't mean to be one more guy who bashes the church, because I do love her. So I'd like to make a differentiation. I believe the church herself is God's idea and is an absolute essential. She's meant to be a countercultural force for good empowered by a loving God. But I think *church culture* can be an unhealthy cyst on the core intentions of God, and the further we stray, the more we bury the real foundation.

One of the symptoms of church culture is our quickness to be a "Good Witness." We have automatic responses to appear content and godly, even when we're not all there inside.

Sometimes at Bible Study, a well-meaning gentleman will say, *"If you don't have joy and peace and compassion in your life, what does that say to others about Jesus?"*

So it's said, "If I really knew God, I should be rejoicing right now."

I understand this sort of thinking. Christians are supposed to look different than everyone else and to have a "reason for our hope." At times our lack of joy isn't good for our brand name, so we conform our faith for sale.

But some days — I just want to flip a table and kick a trashcan and jump out a window and tell everyone that I hate my life right now, and that it probably won't get better if you tell me that I need to be a "better witness." Sometimes life is just too hard to pretend.

Again, this is about making us more human and not less.

I get that we're called to bear fruits and endure patiently and other Christianese things like that, but it sort of shuts down what's really going on in here. When I fake it, I end up feeling like a failure about my failures. I would be thrilled if someone stood up in Bible Study, grabbed a mic, and simply said, *"Life sucks and I hate all of you and I don't know if I believe in God anymore."* At least we can work with that. It's a starting place.

Taking Off The Gloss:
Kill The Poetry

I have to be honest though. I'm still a sucker for inspirational stories. We all are. Some intractable part of us will always be moved by them.

So maybe there's a different way we can tell them.

My first pastor was a great story-teller. He loved the victory stories, too.

He used to tell these testimonies of real people laced with humor and insight, and each time, it would end with the perfect punch-line. You know the kind. At the end of the sermon, you might even bring out the guy who was changed and everyone would clap and cry. I don't mean to sound cynical, because I would always be one of the clappers and criers.

But one story I recall vividly was about a man who was rescued from poverty and given a second chance; he had a difficult childhood, no parents or mentors, and was pulled from his nightmare in a dramatic make-over. Just when I thought this was the ending, my pastor says, "After that, do you know what he did with his life? He ended up turning to crime. He ended up killing someone. He got the death sentence. Because no one taught him a better way."

I remember this story because it was so unlike anything I heard in church before. I liked the sexy stories of redemption. I only approved of a certain amount of tragedy, in just the right size and wrapping. But my pastor suddenly brought the real world into the pulpit, a world of disorder and bleak uncertainty. He didn't try to gloss it over. He wanted us to let go of our pretty picture of progress and recovery.

At the end, he could only conclude that we must help each other climb, and that there will be many setbacks, failures, and wasted second chances. Life is dirty, and our socks will fill with sweat and pebbles. Our spines will bend. Our hands will bleed.

If we're going to move forward, we need to know the path is jagged. There's very little fist-pumping. There will be long nights of cry-face and ugly ranting. Your friends and family will try to understand, but most of the time, you'll be traversing the contours of darkness on your own.

But this is okay.

It's expected.

If you can expect this, you won't be too disappointed when you feel like quitting, because this is how everyone is supposed to feel. You won't be disillusioned when you don't have the Hollywood epiphanies and highlight reels. You'll be braced for impact.

When we finally stop thinking that pain is poetry, we can see it for what it really is: stinky, gross, and horrible. It's then we might truly estimate what we're facing, and how.

My Disability Is Not A Motivation

I just hope we're real about the stories we're telling.

I don't tell many people, but English was not my first language. About 99% of the time, you wouldn't be able to tell, but sometimes it slips and my insecurity spills out sideways.

I've had stage fright since sixth grade. To this day I still get light-headed when I speak in public. I also had a lisp and a stutter, both of which occasionally seep out too. For two years of my childhood, I breathed through a machine for an hour each day, in order to open up my undeveloped lungs. I had asthma and chronic bronchitis. I'm legally blind. I've had hemorrhoids since I was nine. I permanently damaged my lower left back when I was fifteen. I've struggled with depression, including a suicide attempt in 2004. I'm allergic to just about everything: dairy, pollen, bugs, dust, and every single fruit (so I can't eat pineapple pizza or most ice creams). I have scars from all my hive break-outs over the years. I have flat feet. I've never ran over a mile in my life, because I physically cannot. And I know there are millions of others who are afflicted with so much worse.

I was able to get my black belt by eleven years old, but only because my dad pushed me so hard (it also helped that he's a ninth degree black belt and owned several dojos). I can now max out 275 lbs. on the bench-press and part of my job as a pastor is to speak in public several times per week.

Yet I tell you this not because I'm some kind of victorious story and not to brag or to say "You can do it too!" *My disability is not a motivation for some grand story of redemption.* It's not a cute romantic made-for-TV montage. Because, in fact, life is way harder than that. There are many times I wanted to give up because of my physical limitations, or I let them be excuses to stay home and wallow in self-victimizing pity. Anything I achieved was an uphill battle, and still is. None of it came naturally or easily or inherently to my stature.

I could be the positive blogger who says "No matter what! —" but really that would be a lie. Knowing that I will never be fully healthy is psychologically taxing, and some days I grit my teeth and barely get through the day.

Would it be easier if God had made me differently? Of course. I have no illusions about "God held me back for a reason." I can't sugarcoat that with pep-talk which denies the difficulty of our circumstances. I don't want to be a cheap grinning poster boy for a pseudo-inspirational sales pitch.

The one thing I know is that either way, whether we sit down or move forward, *life is pain.*

If I choose to stay home, it will hurt.

If I choose to chase my hopes, it will hurt.

If I choose to feel sorry for myself, it will hurt.

If I choose to stand, clench my fists, grit my teeth, and grab my dreams: it will hurt.

My physical disability is only half the story, because we're all saddled with the same anxiety, second-guessing, and self-doubt. Our brokenness runs deep, and we all work from pain. And it'll hurt anyway.

The last thing I want to do is to inspire you. What I mean is, my little highlight reel at the end of the journey will misinform you about reality. An incomplete inspiration presumes that there are no setbacks, that life is an upward journey that only requires you "try harder." It presumes that all your failures are all your fault, as if you merely didn't try hard enough. It presumes you're only the sum of your abilities and accomplishments.

I want to tell you how it really is.

That even though you and I are a work in progress, it takes *work* and *progress.*

I want to tell you that life is not just a summit, but the whole dang mountain, that it's sweat and stains, and that every victory you've ever heard of was paid by the cost of flesh.

I'm not merely the weaknesses I've overcome. What I am is where I make myself available today.

God help me, God willing, I want to climb this mountain.

"Relying on God has to begin all over again every day as if nothing had yet been done."[13]
— C.S. Lewis

"The pain may never make sense, but the thing to remember is that you survived, and that is reason enough to move on."[14]
— T.B. LaBerge

---

[13] C.S. Lewis, *The Collected Letters of C.S. Lewis, Vol II* (NY: HarperCollins, 1905, 2004), p. 980

[14] http://tblaberge.tumblr.com/post/98978577991

The doctors were sure if I fell asleep, I wouldn't wake up.

It was too late to pump my stomach. Half a bottle of Excedrin. They were about to insert the tube down my throat. Instead they fed me liquid charcoal to neutralize the acid. My vomit was the color of midnight, of tar.

I waited. I fell asleep.

You can feel death, you know. It's like someone is unraveling a thread at the back of your skull, like sinking into yourself. My legs felt like they were dangling in water. My life didn't flash before my eyes. It would've been so easy to keep falling, to sink, to follow the thread to the bottom.

But in that moment, hanging over the abyss — there it was. Not some neon sign or some grand eloquent entrance, not a voice from the rafters, but a simple expression of something beyond this world.

"You're not done yet. You have more. You have Me."

I woke up. I was Baker Act'ed into a mental hospital. I wore someone else's clothes. A man with a clipboard asked me questions about my father. A patient in the next room pulled the fire alarm and tried to jump out the window. Another patient tried to fight me. I was let out after regaining "social acceptability." I lost thirteen pounds in three days and had roomed with others who had far worse problems than I.

Back into the sunlight, I suddenly didn't want to waste my life anymore. I couldn't stand the thought of having died in that hospital bed.

I wanted to believe it all had meaning,

that a purpose awaited me,

that I was made to save a corner of this universe,

that I am much more than what I feel.

It took inches before death to find the beginning of trusting Him. Maybe part of trusting God was trusting that He might actually like me

— not because of what I could do, but simply because I was breathing the air He had whispered into my lungs.

I thought of the verse: It does not profit a man to gain the whole world but lose his soul. If this is true, it means your soul and mine has infinitely more value to God than the whole world. For every person who is tired of living, God says,

You're not done yet.

You have more.

You have Me.

— **J.S.**

CONQUERING THE DRAGON:

The cavernous underbelly of great evil

[CHAPTER 4]

Chapter 4
Conquering The Dragon:
The Cavernous Underbelly of Great Evil

Waking Up To The Monster

In the television show *True Detective,*[15] Detective Rustin Cohle, played by an excellent Matthew McConaughey, despises the random chaos of our lives. He also relishes and revels in his nihilism, as he says, "I thought I was mainlining the secret truth to the universe." He describes the photographs of homicide victims, having to see them over and over, concluding that each person's life that was cut short simply accepted their demise. They finally saw their lives as an illusion, a cruel joke, a fragile vapor. This flicker of hope we each have, he seems to say, is snuffed out when we meet our end. Rust says,

> *"You, yourself, this whole big drama, it was never more than a jerry rig of presumption and dumb will, and you could just let go. To finally know that you didn't have to hold on so tight. To realize that all your life, all your love, all your hate, all your memories, all your pain, it was all the same thing. It was all the same dream, a dream that you had inside a locked room, a dream about being a person, and like a lot of dreams, there's a monster at the end of it."*[16]

---

[15] Just to be clear, I'm not endorsing that you should watch this show. It's full of graphic violence, nudity, cursing, and every scary thing imaginable. This is an issue of Romans 14. If you have serious trigger warnings or a personal vow for family-friendly media, I advise not to watch.

[16] As portrayed by Matthew McConaughey in "True Detective," written by Nic Pizzolatto

I'd imagine that anyone in law enforcement or medical care eventually has to grow jaded to the apparent randomness of suffering. I can't imagine that a doctor or detective would sit still in a sermon without thinking, "This is offensive crap." While the Sunday church service is rocking it out with laser lights and fog machines and subwoofers, there are the disenchanted few in the back row who have seen the cavernous underbelly of great evil.

You don't have to know such pervasive evil to get jaded. It's not always because of a natural disaster or a corporate bad guy. If you've been betrayed in a relationship, if a friend lies to your face, if your hard work was lost, if you've been robbed or slandered or abandoned — you've felt the *unraveling*. Our ideas of safety and shelter are then punctured by suspicion and mistrust. It's a dampening, a dim fog that closes in, like a veil has been pulled through the middle of your vision.

I know we don't like to talk about these things.

But we'll eventually encounter them: so we need to talk about them.

What Kind of God Would Do That?

When I was still a new Christian, my first pastor took our church to a hospital to visit a young boy who had been hospitalized. He had been in a car accident; his mother had died. The boy wasn't any older than ten.

We were only allowed to enter a few at a time. When it was my turn, I went in with my pastor and another church member. When the three of us saw the child, we wept instantly. Here was a scrawny, mangled kid connected to dozens of liquid-filled tubes, a machine doing his breathing, and *half his head* was gone. From his eyebrows up, his skull had been cut off. The machine was so furiously pumping air into his nostrils that the child's entire body was shaking, and another tube was pulling mucus from his lungs. I could not stop weeping. We each held the child and prayed for him through tears, with words that could hardly be uttered.

What could we really say? What words could suffice?

The child eventually died. He never found out his mother had died, too.

I haven't been able to get this image out of my head. I went home that day disturbed. I had so many questions, so many doubts.

Why God? Why like this? What's your plan here? What was the point of this?

No blog posts, no kickstarters, no media coverage.

No heroism, no sacrifice, no stories.

A mother and her child, simply crushed to dust.

—

In an interview on the show "The Meaning of Life," actor Stephen Fry was asked what he would say to God if he met Him. Stephen responded,

"I'll say, 'Bone cancer in children, what's that about? How dare you? How dare you create a world in which there is such misery that's not our fault.' It's not right. It's utterly, utterly evil. Why should I respect a capricious, mean-minded, stupid God who creates a world which is so full of injustice and pain?

"The God who created this universe, if he created this universe, is quite clearly a maniac, an utter maniac, totally selfish. We have to spend our lives on our knees thanking him. What kind of God would do that? Yes, the world is very splendid, but it also has in it insects whose whole life cycle is to burrow into the eyes of children and make them blind, to eat outward from the eyes. Why? Why did you do that to us? You could have easily made a creation in which that didn't exist. It is simply not acceptable.

"Atheism is not just about not believing there's a god. On the assumption there is one, what kind of God is he? It's perfectly apparent that he is monstrous, utterly monstrous, and deserves no respect. The moment you banish him, your life becomes simpler, purer, cleaner, more worth living in my opinion."

This is also similar to a monologue made by a fictional character from *Orange Is The New Black*. The protagonist says what many of us have already been thinking.

"I can't pretend to believe in something that I don't, and I don't ... See this isn't doubts. I believe in science. I believe in evolution. I believe in Nate Silver, Neil deGrasse Tyson, and Christopher Hitchens although I do admit he could be kind of an a__hole. I can't get behind a supreme being that weighs in on the Tony Awards while a million people get whacked by machetes. I don't believe a billion Indians are going to hell, I don't think that we get cancer to learn life lessons, and I don't believe that people die young because God needs another angel. I think it's bullsh_t. And on some level I think we all know that, don't you? Look I understand that religion makes it easier to deal with all the random shitty things that happen to us, and I wish I could get on that ride. I'm sure I would be happier, but I can't. Feelings aren't enough. I need it to be real."

The thing is, I probably know all the right theology to respond. I know the proper responses for a formal debate in an air-conditioned room with our calm, collected voices. I can tell you about God's Sovereignty and supralapsarianism and all His mysterious ways.

But when you take a long look at the world: we've all felt this *angry*. We've all wanted to look up to the Heavens and say, *"How dare you?"* In each of our minds, we have a list of questions we would like to ask God when we meet Him. I'm guessing the biggest question has to be:

"If you're so good, then why? Why did you ___?"

Jerry DeWitt, a pastor who turned atheist after twenty-five years of ministry, says the day he lost faith is when he could no longer comfort a grieving friend. He says, "Who on this planet has any idea what I'm going through?"[17]

The Problem of Evil hasn't been adequately answered by the greatest philosophers of history, and I'm not going to be the one to unlock the mystery, either. Even a solid answer couldn't satisfy you in your suffering, no matter how much it makes logical sense to your brain. The very best theology on God can be deconstructed by continual reductionism, until you're left with nothing but an "utter maniac" who is "utterly monstrous" and "deserves no respect."

But one thing I've found is: perhaps those who would say *"How dare you"* are closer to God than they think. It's true: *"Feelings aren't enough. I need it to be real."*

Maybe they're getting at the heart of God much better than you and I.

---

[17] http://www.nytimes.com/2012/08/26/magazine/from-bible-belt-pastor-to-atheist-leader.html

Be Frustrated, Be Furious

Shortly after I visited the hospital of that young child, I went to a service at a mega-church where the pastor preached on pain. I was ready to roll my eyes. More platitudes, more flailing to make order out of chaos. I didn't want to hear this.

The pastor spoke of a young man who was engaged to be married, but then his fiancé was struck by lightning and killed. A senseless tragedy, a supposed Act of God.

The young man had told the pastor:

"I know God is teaching me something here, but you know what — *damn this lesson.* Damn this lesson to hell."

The pastor didn't try to clean this up. He let it hang there, a floating question mark carving the air. This was an uncomfortable space, like two fingers gripping the edge of a rotten cliff — but here, I found the beginning of unclenching my frustration.

I found that maybe yelling at the chaos was the point. Maybe floating in uncertainty is the first step out of apathy. It meant we cared that things were so unjust. We knew the universe had gone wrong, and we were right to be so frustrated and furious. It meant I could say, *Damn this lesson,* because we don't need one. We can scream into the abyss, because this in itself is the start of fighting the dark. It meant we weren't screaming alone, because we're all clutching this ledge together, asking why and staring into our questions.

This didn't make things okay.

As I once read, *"You do have to learn to live with this, but that doesn't mean you have to like it."*[18]

---

[18] John S. Feinberg, *Suffering and the Goodness of God* (IL: Crossway, 2008) p. 224

This pointed to the fact that *I knew things weren't okay, that something is horribly wrong — and that we want something outside this to exist.* We might not know where it comes from, but we know we want heroism to win, for chaos to have a consummation, for everything to be okay.

We become detectives and doctors because we still believe that life needs to be put right again. Our normal is darkness, but we know it *shouldn't* be. We're sucked into this unwinding entropy of sand through our fingers, but we fight so hard against it. We put on wings to fight gravity. We pack sutures to bind up wounds. We offer shoulders to pick up the weary.

I don't know why this boy or this man's fiancé had to die such terrible deaths. I can't ask why. I don't think any line of reasoning would satisfy us. I'll question it all the way to heaven. I only know that I'm mad, and grieving, and that all of me is shouting against the dark.

The Forever Empty: Dancing Around The Dark

This "chaos" is not just great evil or everyday suffering. It's not always prompted by anything that happens around us.

There's also a stirring, palpable itch inside us.

When we sit still for too long, there's an unbearable, anguished silence in the deepest floor of our gut that claws at the back of our throats. It's a churning void that you only experience in deep quiet. It's a mix of different things. It could be the pounding march of the clock, each irreversible grain of sand shutting the door behind you. It could be the simple cost of living, the awareness that by being alive, we have no choice but to die. It could be the endless appetite inside, the uneasy quest of finding satisfaction in a phantom life that eludes us, never quenched, but only dulled. You've felt this, too. Without warning, we're struck with a sudden bolt of Existential Panic that breaks the spell of our self-importance, and we realize how quickly our significance is dashed to nothing.

At three in the morning when you're watching your ceiling fan spin: you feel it. You wonder. You want to know what this is really all about, this eye-blink of an existence, and your chest is squeezed into breathless terror.

Could it be for nothing?

In an interview with Conan O'Brien, comedian and actor Louis C.K. talked about why he hates cell phones. In his usual cutting delivery, Louis got to the bottom of our unwillingness to be honest with ourselves.

> *"You need to build an ability to just be yourself and not be doing something. That's what the phones are taking away, is the ability to just sit there. That's being a person. Because underneath everything in your life there is that thing, that empty — forever empty. That knowledge that it's all for nothing and that you're alone. It's down there, and sometimes when things clear away, you're not watching anything, you're in your car, and you start going, 'Oh no, here it comes, that I'm alone.' It starts to visit on you. Just this sadness. Life is tremendously sad, just by being in it."*
>
> *"... That's why we text and drive. I look around, pretty much 100 percent of the people driving are texting. Everybody's murdering each other with their cars. But people are willing to risk taking a life and ruining their own because they don't want to be alone for a second,*

because it's so hard. I go, 'Oh, I'm getting sad, got to get the phone and write 'Hi' to like fifty people.' ... Then I said, 'You know what, don't. Just be sad ... Stand in the way of it, let it hit you like a truck.'

"I let it come, and I just started to feel 'Oh my God,' and I pulled over and I just cried like a b_tch. I cried so much, and it was beautiful. Sadness is poetic. You're lucky to live sad moments. Then I had happy feelings. Because when you let yourself feel sad, your body has antibodies, it has happiness that comes rushing in to meet the sadness. So I was grateful to feel sad, and then I met it with true, profound happiness. It was such a trip."[19]

You and I know the "forever empty" he's talking about. He says it's the fear that "it's all for nothing and that you're alone."

It's the uncertainty of a fragile life.

That we're stuck within time and we fall off to nothing. It's the terrifying possibility that nothing has a rhyme or reason. It's the inevitability that everything will end in death and decay.

Every year, you look in the mirror and you see it happening. Nothing will stop it.

As Shakespeare said in one of his most over-used passages,

"Life's but a walking shadow; a poor player,
that struts and frets his hour upon the stage,
and then is heard no more: it is a tale told by an idiot,
full of sound and fury, signifying nothing."[20]

The larger point is that we avoid confronting this emptiness in ourselves. We'll do anything to run from the uncertainty. We're constantly masking the panic inside. We have so many coping

---

[19] https://www.youtube.com/watch?v=5HbYScltf1c
[20] William Shakespeare, *Macbeth,* Act 5, Scene 5, 19-28

mechanisms. You know what I mean. It's why we latch onto a To-Do List. It's why we have text message madness. It's why we jump from channel to channel, song to song, one video to the next, down the wiki-hole, religion to alcohol, job to girlfriend, haircut to hair color, with little space between.

I'm sure none of this is new to you and I'm not trying to revolutionize your thinking. Any college student who's been to Philosophy 101 can tell you what I'm telling you. But that's exactly my point. Even intellectualism can be a smokescreen to run from the hard questions. To formulize our fear into academia doesn't solve a thing. We're so afraid of depth that we'll find any possible way to whistle past the graveyard.

Many of us never dare to "let it hit you like a truck." It's too threatening and too horrible, to consider that all this is for nothing and that we're simply alone.

Here's what I'm betting though.

I'm betting that our propensity to deny our darkness, both inside and out, points to a clue about reality. *The very fact that we're so disturbed by our emptiness could mean that emptiness is a flaw and not the norm.* We want to know everything matters and that there are answers — and we would hate to find out that it doesn't.

In the silence, I learn who I really am. I learn that I need help, and not from my phone and connected media and the buzz of the "like" button. I need the help that only comes with the quiet digestion of my imperfection. Silence is sometimes our only honesty.

It's when we encounter such unplugged loneliness that we can no longer deny the existential questions. As Louis said, we have "antibodies." The questions surface, the fingernails scratching the roof of your mouth, and we taste the smallest hint of *something else.*

When life hits us, whether from inside or out there, we encounter the frail, fragile mortality of our walking shadows. "It is a tale told by an idiot." But inside this maddening sadness, there's a lingering rebellion that we don't want it to be.

It's what C.S. Lewis called the "megaphone." It's awakening to *something more.*

Wishful Thinking:
The Argument Against Desire

I know when I say, *There has to be something else,* I'm potentially jumping to a cliché. I don't want to make it that easy.

Before I go on, let's say that my hope for "something else" is wishful thinking.

In perhaps his most famous quote, C.S. Lewis said, *"If I find in myself desires which nothing in this world can satisfy, the only logical explanation is that I was made for another world."*

This is known as the *Argument from Desire.* It's an absolutely wonderful thought. Lewis says that since we have hunger, it necessarily points to a thing that exists called food. For thirst, we have water, and for exhaustion, we have sleep. He expands upon this in his work *The Abolition of Man,* in which he says sunsets and ice cream evoke a higher beauty that goes beyond the thing itself, all the way up to divinity.

I really love this logic because I want my longing to be longing for something that exists. But I also know this logic has holes.

The Argument from Desire could really be inherited genetic material or an evolutionary trait that helped us survive. Just because my feelings point somewhere doesn't mean that it's pointing anywhere. My desire for unicorns and superheroes doesn't make them real. Sunsets might point to a divine artist, but hurricanes and earthquakes would point to a planetary vandal. There are plenty of cultures that have a different consensus on what is good in and of itself. Some tribes sacrifice children to malevolent gods; the Mbenzele Pygmies in the Congo think the soundtrack for *Psycho* is a pop song.[21] And to make this leap from "desire" to a Christian God is far too much of a leap.

I can't speak to every particular association of good or bad.

I'm sure there are genetics involved.

I'm sure there are better arguments against the Argument from Desire.

I don't think a desire for something greater than this world proves that a supernatural world exists.

I just know that the desire itself *does* exist. It's absurd that we even have a thing called "wishful thinking" at all. It's expressed everywhere, in paintings and poetry and pop songs and the flavors of ice cream. We might wish for different things, but we do wish for them. The power to imagine what isn't there is such a weird, wild human ability with no utilitarian function. At the same time, without it, life isn't really life either.

---

[21] http://www.npr.org/blogs/goatsandsoda/2015/01/09/375418410/why-pygmies-arent-scared-by-the-psycho-theme

I'm not arguing that "wishful thinking" makes anything true. It's just weird that we would wish for anything, regardless of what it is. It's weird that we would desire to argue against the Argument from Desire. It's strange that we paint the sunset and wait for the sunrise. It's strange that so many of our heroes look the same, and so do many of our villains.

I think Lewis could've shortened the quote to: *I find in myself desires.* That's the surprise.

The desire for some things to be true and other things to be untrue does not prove a single thing. But the desire itself remains.

We go on living like life has meaning, even as we curse at that which appears meaningless. We long for better even as we curse at our longing. At some point, I stretch these two extremes so far that it feels like I'm cutting down the very branch I'm sitting on.

And what about the unthinkable possibility that it's going somewhere? What if our desires are really fighting for something? Maybe not. Maybe it's all wishful thinking. **But you would have to fight even harder to wish for nothing.**

So I choose to take my desire at face value. It's there, it's pesky, it's some days unbearable: and it's not going away.

"If the whole universe has no meaning, we should never have found out that it has no meaning: just as, if there were no light in the universe and therefore no creatures with eyes, we should never know it was dark. Dark would be without meaning."

— C.S. Lewis

"Desire, a function central to all human experience, is the desire for nothing nameable. And at the same time this desire lies at the origin of every variety of animation. If being were only what it is, there wouldn't even be room to talk about it."[22]

— Jacques Lacan

"If something is going to happen to me, I want to be there."[23]
— Albert Camus

"I Don't Want Happily Ever After"
The Perpetual State of Unresolved Tension

Let's take the opposite view for a moment. Let's say there's nothing else but darkness and the dust. Let's say that the gloomy artists are right: life is pointless and people are selfish and there's nothing more.

The news can back this up. Many of us are profoundly stirred by a nihilistic story with an unhappy ending. I think we like this kind of stuff because it feels very real and relevant.

But of all the things we desire to be true: secretly, I doubt we want this one to be true.

Here's what I mean. The most popular podcast of all time, *Serial,* covered a real crime that took place in 1999 in which a high school senior Hae Min Lee was found dead in a park in Maryland.[24]

---

[22] Jacques Lacan, *The Seminar of Jacques Lacan: Book II* (Cambridge: Cambridge University Press, 1988) p.223

[23] Albert Camus, *The Stranger* (Cambridge: Cambridge University Press, 1988, 2004) p. 113

[24] This is a great podcast (in so far as such things can be "great"), but I strongly urge a trigger warning for the graphic nature of the show. It involves real people and a real murder, with many unfiltered descriptions and language.

Her ex-boyfriend, Adnan Syed, has been in jail for the crime ever since, but has protested his innocence for the last decade and a half. The podcast has over forty-million downloads and provoked amateur online sleuths to solve her murder.

The narrator of the series, Sarah Koenig, promised an ending in the twelfth and final episode of the show. Yet her ending didn't wrap up like many thought it would, either with the "real killer" or some new finding. It simply ended with her opinion. Social media took Koenig to task for the anti-climax, such as remarking the finale was "an odd, inconclusive curveball" and it had become a "tawdry and voyeuristic exercise."[25]

Of course, that's real life. There are no clean endings. I didn't expect one, and it would've been even more "tawdry" to try for it. But I understood the general public reaction to the show's finale. I don't think it was because the narrator over-promised, but because *we intrinsically demand the pieces to pull together.* We know that even if real life doesn't always work out, that *it should work out somehow.*

Pop culture will continually have us believe that we like gritty art, and a part of us loves it. But a deeper part of us resists it — and I think we need to listen in to this deeper pulse.

The grim pessimism in a lot of books and movies feels realistic because we're trying to be brutally honest and to relate to each other. It's *artistic.* I'm totally into that too. Those end-of-the-world apocalypse stories are fascinating because you see the fully exposed depths of our depravity, and underneath our barely polite skin is a cauldron of violence and survival. In those miserable poems and ambiguous endings and Poe-ish nightmare

---

[25] http://www.theguardian.com/tv-and-radio/tvandradioblog/2014/dec/18/serial-final-episode-12-podcast-review-an-odd-inconclusive-curveball

landscapes, we understand the pain. It's familiar, even comfortable. I feel validated in other peoples' despair.

But really —

No one ever lives this way for too long. Even the *very idea that we can relate to pain is also finding hope in the narrowest doorway.* We want to know we're not alone in this.

We say that a cheerful ending in a dark movie is "Hollywood-izing" or somehow "rings false," but I think we just say that because it makes us look more sophisticated. We like the dark comic book movie because it seems more "mature," when really, such grit wears thin. We need *The Avengers* to wash down *The Dark Knight.* We're quickly peer-pressured out of being the optimistic sap who still has hope for a brighter world. We prefer the main character to die in some horrible Greek tragedy of hubris-like proportions — only because we're forced by postmodern coolness to say so.

I just find that pessimism is too easy and too lazy. It simply accepts the world the way it is — when we're afraid to admit that we just don't want to work to reverse the entropy. The world is the way it is because we keep saying, "This is the way it is." Optimism has become the repressed mainstream nerd at the back of hipster parties.

Villainy has become a cool commodity, but really it's just exposing us as couch potatoes. If we parrot this non-philosophy of circular nihilism, we isolate ourselves behind locked doors to forfeit the effort of rolling up our sleeves and tackling our messy community. We can then call love "cheesy" or "corny" or "tacky" or "passé." We get to wallow in complaints and drown in self-pity. We get to call complacency "being real."

Yet when we see true evil rear its ugly head — slavery, persecution, discrimination, extermination — then sitting on the sidelines is just as evil. It's not artistic. It's not avant-garde. It's just unoriginal.

What's tough is staying hopeful in a hostile world. What impresses me is when people stay compassionate in a conniving world of thieves, thugs, and philanderers. What moves me is self-sacrifice for the unworthy. That's the real art. It's to acknowledge the darkness of our surroundings and being reckless anyway. It's to paint a sunrise with a dirty brush, to speak the colors of beauty through broken lips, to remember a long-ago time of untainted harmony.

I know that not everything has a happily-ever-after. We do hurt, a lot. There are lifelong battles and unconquerable defeats and irreversible losses. There is, at times, unresolved tension that remains unresolved.

Yet our bold response to all these things can show a reservoir of strength we never knew we had.

Our daily victories build scars that build stories that build bridges to broken hearts.

Our boldness shows we don't need to lose ourselves in loss, that we don't need to fall apart when everything else does.

The dark can make us more human, and not less.

In our outright rebellion against apathy, we find a flash of divinity. We find a story better than the childish bleakness of tragedy, but instead the mature growth of comedy, where we have the humility to laugh at ourselves. We find hope in pain together. Maybe even the hope that there's an ever-after. We don't have to hope in solitude.

And maybe we can even cheer up a little.

"Laughter is the evidence that we're still here, the proof that our tragedies will not define us forever. Laughter is the language of the survivor."[26]
— Josh Riebock

—

Here's why I think *Serial* was so popular.

Here's why I think all these heroic stories are popular.

When the question of Adnan Syed's innocence was raised as an actual question, millions of listeners tried to investigate the crime for themselves. If the court missed something, we wanted to know.

Justice had to win. If an innocent man was guilty and a guilty man was free, this couldn't be left alone. The very *possibility* that we had wronged an innocent person evoked the hero in all of us. Maybe, one of us could be the one who cracks the case. One of us could figure out who did it. The hero would be hailed.

We know that hundreds, maybe thousands of people have gotten away with terrible things. We also know that innocent men and women are imprisoned all the time. You and I have been wrongly accused, too. We've been hurt, and someone got away with it. Or we hurt others, and no one ever knew. None of this sits well with us. For me, I lose sleep over it. I shout at a world gone wrong and a heart gone bad. I see the enemy in the news just as much as I see it in myself.

As far gone as our world might be, we have a sense that *wrong must be vanquished* and *wrong must be atoned for.*

---

[26] Josh Riebock, *Heroes and Monsters* (MI: Baker Books, 2012) p. 163

I am a shouter at the dark.

I have a feeling you are, too.

We inherently want to conquer the dragon.

But very possibly, we already know a dragon conqueror.

And very possibly, we have the conqueror's fingerprints beating in our hearts.

"Since it is so likely that children will meet cruel enemies, let them at least have heard of brave knights and heroic courage."[27]

— C.S. Lewis

———

Detective Rustin, after a near-death experience in the final episode of *True Detective*, opens up to his friend Detective Marty at the hospital.

Up to this point, Rustin had only been spewing nihilistic proclamations about the world. Even when they catch up to the killer, there are still larger players in the crimes, still loose threads, and it hardly feels like the ending we've been waiting for.

But Rust's final dialogue, while not a happy conclusion, is perhaps the surprise twist that no one saw coming.

Rust: *There was a moment, I know, when I was under in the dark, that something, whatever I'd been reduced to, not even consciousness, just a vague awareness in the dark. I could feel my definitions fading. And beneath that darkness there was another kind, it was deeper, warm, like a substance. I could feel man, I knew, I knew my daughter waited for*

---

[27] C.S. Lewis, *On Stories: And Other Essays on Literature* (FL: Harcourt, 1966, 1982) p. 39

me there. So clear. I could feel her. I could feel the peace of my Pop, too. It was like I was part of everything that I have ever loved, and we were all, the three of us, just fading out. And all I had to do was let go, man. And I did. I said, "Darkness, yeah," and I disappeared. But I could still feel her love there. Even more than before. Nothing but that love. And then I woke up. I tell you Marty, I've been up in that room looking out those windows every night here just thinking, it's just one story. The oldest.

Marty: *What's that?*

Rust: *Light versus dark.*

Marty: *Well, I know we ain't in Alaska, but it appears to me that the dark has a lot more territory.*

Rust: *Yeah, you're right about that ... You're looking at it wrong, the sky thing.*

Marty: *How's that?*

Rust: *Well, once there was only dark. You ask me, the light's winning.*

"Fairy tales, then, are not responsible for producing in children fear, or any of the shapes of fear; fairy tales do not give the child the idea of the evil or the ugly; that is in the child already, because it is in the world already. Fairy tales do not give the child his first idea of bogey. What fairy tales give the child is his first clear idea of the possible defeat of bogey. The baby has known the dragon intimately ever since he had an imagination. What the fairy tale provides for him is a St. George to kill the dragon.

"Exactly what the fairy tale does is this: it accustoms him for a series of clear pictures to the idea that these limitless terrors had a limit, that these shapeless enemies have enemies in the knights of God, that there is something in the universe more mystical than darkness, and stronger than strong fear."[28]

— G. K. Chesterton

Sam: *It's like in the great stories, Mr. Frodo. The ones that really mattered. Full of darkness and danger they were. And sometimes you didn't want to know the end. Because how could the end be happy? How could the world go back to the way it was when so much bad had happened? But in the end, it's only a passing thing, this shadow. Even darkness must pass. A new day will come. And when the sun shines it will shine out the clearer. Those were the stories that stayed with you. That meant something, even if you were too small to understand why. But I think, Mr. Frodo, I do understand. I know now. Folk in those stories had lots of chances of turning back, only they didn't. They kept going, because they were holding on to something.*
Frodo: *What are we holding onto, Sam?*
Sam: *That there's some good in this world, Mr. Frodo, and it's worth fighting for.*
— The Lord of the Rings: The Two Towers[29]

---

[28] G.K. Chesterton, *Tremendous Trifles* (NY: Dodd, Mead, and Co. 1909) p. 130
[29] *The Lord of the Rings: The Two Towers*. Film adaptation by Dir. Peter Jackson, original by J.R.R. Tolkien. New Line Cinema, 2002

LIVE LONG AND PROSPER:

Hijacking (and reclaiming) Jeremiah 29:11

[INTERLUDE 1]

Interlude 1

Live Long and Prosper:
Hijacking (And Reclaiming) Jeremiah 29:11

Lord Robitussin:
Over-The-Counter God

Dear friend: I want to talk with you about a verse that might have absolutely crushed you. It's given many of us hope and peace, but for so many others, it might have bludgeoned you with the sour taste of false promise.

That verse, of course, is Jeremiah 29:11. It says:

"For I know the plans I have for you," declares the LORD, "plans to prosper you and not to harm you, plans to give you hope and a future."

Let's consider how weird this verse really is.

If I told you, "I got plans for you, not to hurt you but to help you" — you would probably say, "Is something wrong? Are you mad at me? You wanted to hurt me?"

If you're a parent, try it with your kids. Watch them slowly back out of the room with their hands up. Try it with your friends. They might fight you.

I think this verse is often shared with good intentions, about a God who is promising you a brighter future. But right up front,

I have to apologize, because it's guys like me who made this verse too easy and too soft, who over-promised and under-delivered on a pocket-sized, remote-controlled version of God.

It's guys like me who consolidated our entire theology into this single verse and told you with both thumbs up, "God has an amazing plan for your life!" — all while your entire life was crumbling around you in a smoldering heap. And I'm sorry. We baited you and lured you with a God like Robitussin, an over-the-counter cure for your sniffles and scraped knees.

Please know that I don't ever want to make you afraid of Jeremiah 29:11. I don't want to say that you've been using it wrong or that I got it totally right. I just want us to get the whole picture. Preachers like me gave you half the story.

I told you about a God who would change your situation if you trusted Him, and when nothing changed, you rightfully rejected a simplified God.

I'm really very sorry.

No one is more sorry about this than me.

I have a friend Grace, who suffers from a genetic disease called MELAS that has afflicted her with uncontrollable seizures, paralyzed muscles, vision loss, multiple strokes, and slurred speech. The disease is progressive and terminal. She began experiencing seizures in middle school and will probably not make it to thirty years of age. When she turned eighteen, we held a Prom Dance for her in her hospital room.

My friend Grace is a Christian, meaning she believes in the work and person of Jesus. If I were to tell her, "God has plans to prosper you and not to harm you, plans to give you hope and a future" — she would nod and agree, but only because she has to. Underneath the assent would be some desperate questions.

Is this really God's plan to prosper me?

Didn't God say He wouldn't harm me?

Is this part of God's hope and future?

I don't mean to use my friend's illness to make a point. I'm wrestling with these very same questions. There are just too many Bible verses that seem to say, "God is in control, you have a bright future ahead, He has great plans for you," but it's patronizing when life falls apart. Not everyone gets better. Not everyone finds relief. Verses like these are abstract and ethereal, like God is only talking about the afterlife.

I wonder if we're forcing these verses to say something they don't.

We can smile and nod and agree when we read them, but only with a grim endurance. At worst, these verses are mocking us, like everyone else got in with God except *me*.

I keep thinking, *"What about my friend Grace? What about those irreversible situations? What about those complicated, fractured, upended families that will never be okay?"*

It's a constant nagging, the *What-About.*

Taking Back Jeremiah 29:11, Way Back

Here's the thing. **No one would've found Jeremiah 29:11 more ridiculous than the original recipients who read them.**

About 2600 years ago, Jeremiah wrote this letter to the Israelites who had been captured and uprooted to a pagan nation called Babylon. This enslavement was called the *Babylonian Captivity.*

Imagine armed men breaking into your room right now, at your local Starbucks, at your school or workplace or church, and dragging you through the streets as they torched every building and home and grocery store on the way to a different country. You're not sure if you'll ever see your family or your city again. You're dumped into a new school where you have to learn the language and customs and fashion and economy of the land. Your money has the face of the president who enacted this siege against you. You're not allowed to practice your faith or speak your native language or eat your favorite foods; you'll never have the full rights that are accorded to every other citizen. You're marked a slave, segregated to the worst part of this new city, and you're the first to take the frontlines of any new war that's waged by your captors. Your children are often displaced to a new home to be slaves and soldiers, too. They'll be taught that your captors are gods, that your home country is the enemy, and that your faith is a myth. It will only be a few years until your language, your culture, and your memories are stamped out.

It's within this awful, degrading, humiliation that Jeremiah says, *God has plans to prosper you, not to harm you, but to give you a hope and a future.*

This is why God has to say, "I'm not trying to harm you," because every Israelite during the Captivity was already beat down and battered. The harm had been done.

Jeremiah wasn't promising a good situation, but speaking into a bad one.

When God said, "I have plans to give you a hope and a future," it's possible that the Israelites in the seventh century BC believed this. Some of them held on for a few years, even. They had been delivered from oppression before, most dramatically by Moses, with special effects and a severed sea. They knew the stories of Elijah and Elisha, who had called down fire on a mountaintop and brought back the dead. Maybe the Israelites waited for a king like David, who would liberate them from the evil grip of Babylon.

But year after year, I'm sure they lost faith in the God who had a "plan."

Year after year, I'm sure you've heard this verse drop like an anvil, all-too-loud with the subtlety of a sledgehammer. You brought friends to church who were looking for something more, but this verse only reinforced the belief that the Christian faith was simplistic, stilted, and out of touch. Some of us hear this verse now and *cringe*.

The Israelites probably cringed, too. These words from Jeremiah the Prophet, a voice-box from God, must've been a sad, sick joke.

The Israelites had even more reason to doubt Jeremiah than we do.

You probably haven't been in a situation as extreme as this one, but we've all experienced this uncontrollable kind of suffering before. We're held captive to our situation. We can do nothing. We can change nothing. We're stuck.

Yet the Israelites had one major advantage.

They didn't split Jeremiah's words into chapters and verses: they saw it in whole. The addition of chapters and verses in Scripture didn't happen for another 1800 years. The Israelites would've read Jeremiah's words in totality, with no punctuation, as a holistic story.

In other words, it's not that we've read too much into Jeremiah 29:11 — it's that we've gotten too little. There's so much richness, depth, and power in this passage that we've merely relegated it to a "better life." To simply say that "God will turn it around" isn't going far enough.

Perhaps you saw this coming, but ***without context, there is no content.***

The next two verses after Jeremiah 29:11 say:

12 Then you will call upon me and come and pray to me, and I will listen to you. 13 You will seek me and find me when you seek me with all your heart.

God is not giving an answer to their situation. God tells them, "I have plans for you," and it's followed by:

Call on God, pray to Him, and seek Him with all your heart.

When we put these verses together in logical order, God's Plan for us is simple: *Call on Him.* The amazing plan that He has for you is: *Seek Him with all your heart.*

The plans here do not answer the *What-About?*

These plans are pointing to *What-About-Now?* They do not point to the reason for your hurt, but to the resources to endure.

Before you say, "That's it?" — let's think of the Israelites in Babylon.

As Jeremiah wrote this letter, he knew they were in for the darkest leg of their journey. The Israelites had zero options. Escape would lead to death in the wilderness. Rebellion would lead to execution. Complacency would lead to no provisions for their family. Complying with the Babylonians would be a shameful surrender of their own faith and a capitulation to an oppressive tyranny. Their diagnosis was terminal.

Jeremiah had to give them something: not a pick-me-up cliché to mentally rearrange their feelings, but a *choice in a choiceless situation*. They needed internal liberation while waiting for external freedom.

The best thing Jeremiah can say to them, as given by God, is to **call on God**. He wouldn't have written this with a smile; he was not a stranger to their situation. Jeremiah was with them. He wasn't speaking vain, sugary words to inspire them for a day. It wouldn't work. I believe he was pointing to something deeper.

The Hebrew word for "call out" in Jeremiah 29:12 also means to *cry, scream,* or *shout.* It also means to *invite* or to *summon,* and Jeremiah adds, *with all your heart.* In 1 Kings 18, Elijah the prophet calls out to God, expecting Him to show up. It's the same word. It's to expel the brunt force of your entire being in a particular direction, to become a part of something outside you.

Here in this simple passage and elsewhere in the Bible, we're told an existing truth.

We're already calling out to something in our hurt.

We're inviting something to fill the fractured places.

You and I do this all the time.

Think of when you're physically hurt. Your knee buckles or you stub your toe or you bump your head. All your focus and energy and attention will rush to that point of pain. Sometimes you fall over or you rub your wound or you take a seat. Pain provokes us towards an immediate remedy, whether it's to lean on a wall or to ask for help.

In suffering, we want to move closer to the people who are wise and stable and strong. We stay with friends who can handle our frustration. We move closer to the ones who won't shame us or belittle our problems. We remember the ones who saw us throw a fit and never judged us. We look for a vault to vent, a pillar to lean on, an ear to hear us. We seek both rest and resolution. We're already seeking.

Jeremiah is giving us an underlying description of how we work.

When trouble comes, we call out to something. It's not a matter of *if*, but how. We want stability and balance and justice. And the *something* we find will define our direction in the middle of the mess.

Who you call in your pain defines where your pain will take you.

The thing we choose to call out to will shape where we go from here.

Whether you want to or not, you're responding to pain somehow.

I believe God wants to help you with the *how*.

He knows that we'll be tempted to call on the wrong remedy.

Why Didn't It Say Something Else?

Maybe none of this sounds very profound or practical.

"So we just pray? We just become a Christian?"

The Israelites might have also shrugged this off or gotten mad. We don't like this sort of advice because it sounds obvious or ordinary. It's 101. But I don't think it's advice. Jeremiah was smarter than that and so were the Israelites. We only need to consider the alternatives.

When I get stuck on the meaning of a certain Bible passage, I try to ask, *Why didn't it say something else?*

Jeremiah could've said, "Call out to your friend with all your heart."

This could work for a while and we do need community. I highly recommend going to your friends when you're hurting. Your church is a valuable shelter of counseling and fellowship. But: friends cannot be an inexhaustible supply of wisdom and company. I'm sure your friends wish they could always be there for you, but our friends are just people, too. They get tired, they have bad days, they have their own hurts, just like you and me. They cannot be everything we need them to be.

Jeremiah could've said, "Call out to your achievements and success."

This is actually very helpful. Some of us never pat ourselves on the back for the good things we've done; we concentrate too much on our mistakes and failures and what went wrong. You don't give yourself enough credit. You've done a lot better than you think. But: investing your entire worth into your accomplishments is a never-ending competition. Your success is too easily collapsible. You either reach for the glory days of your past or an idealistic future version of yourself that never comes. Our success cannot be everything we need it to be.

You see where I'm going with this. Jeremiah could've said, "Call out to your spouse. Call out to your one night stand. Call out to your pills. Call out to your porn. Call out to your vacation and quick thrills and reputation and networking and good looks and temper tantrums and gossip and cynicism and paranoia."

I know I sound like an old-fashioned preacher when I talk about it this way. You've probably heard all this before. *What's with you preachers and always fighting temptation?* But I also want to tell you that these responses are perfectly natural. Almost no one instinctively "calls on God." Me neither. We run to easy pleasure to escape the pain. It's nearly impossible to stay with God in the Captivity. I'm not shaming you for that. I'm not saying that you messed up God's plan.

When you and I are hurt, we run to a release, a relief, a refuge.

Why do we do this?

Because we're always looking for wholeness in our hurt. We chase after peace in our pain. We want things the way they used to be, or we want things restored. The root of this desire isn't wrong — but when it turns selfish and sour, it can produce some very toxic fruit. We end up hurting others or hurting ourselves. This is where God wants to protect you.

As you've heard, *Hurt people hurt people.*

In *A Grace Disguised,* Jerry Sittser talks about the various responses to the "silent scream of pain." On September 27th, 1991, Jerry lost three generations of his family in a car accident: his mother, his wife, and one of his daughters. I don't mean to diminish his life or his family into a single sentence. As he says himself, "Some experiences are so terrible that they defy description."[30] I can't imagine the pain he still feels to this day, and I cannot do justice to his story except that you would read it yourself.

In the earliest moments of his loss, Jerry knew he had a choice to "run from the loss or face it as best I could." He writes, "I decided from that point on to walk into the darkness rather than try to outrun it, to let my experience of loss take me on a

---

[30] Jerry Sittser, *A Grace Disguised* (MI: Zondervan, 1995) p.11

journey wherever it would lead."[31] The journey, of course, felt impossible.

He writes about his initial responses: denial of emotions, overhauling his life, indulging in addictions, taking revenge, and cursing at God. He felt that he almost *had* to go through these stages. In the end, he writes,

> *"These initial responses to loss are natural, powerful, and even legitimate. They send a signal that something is desperately wrong in our lives ... [But] these responses, however natural, can deceive us, appearing to provide a way of escape from the problem rather than points of entry into the problem. We must therefore pay attention to them but not fool ourselves into thinking that they are merely stages on our way out of the predicament ... The problem with viewing these avenues of escape as stages is that it raises the false expectation that we go through them only once."[32]*

In other words, our responses to pain are always natural, but they always get us stuck. They continually turn inward and selfish and never satisfy. These things we call out to will eventually *consume more energy than they create.* They consume us even more than the pain itself. I don't want you to get stuck in this. I don't want you to be deceived. Some of this might be okay for a while, but I don't want it to be the running theme of your life. I don't want it to *run* your life.

You know how it goes. Some of us run to thrills or pills or porn. We have fantasy relationships with the next door neighbor or the next trending celebrity. We're constantly daydreaming of another marriage, a different church, a better job. We emotionally

---

31 Ibid., 33-34
32 Ibid., 50-51

cheat on our relationships and steal idealism by romanticizing someone else's life.

I know a lot about this one. My parents divorced on my fourteenth birthday. When I was sixteen, I became addicted to strip clubs. When I was eighteen, I was drunk almost every weekend. I ran after girls and ran from the police. There are large periods of time that I don't remember in college. Ten years ago, a girl that I was living with cheated on me twice, so I swallowed half a bottle of pills to end my life.

I was all about escape. You've been there, too.

I've seen dear friends allow a terrible season of life to turn them just as terrible, by either totally shutting down or acting out — and they become miserable. They had a valid reason to be bitter, but this bitterness wasn't worked out like a flu. It set in like poison. And pain continued to perpetuate pain. At first they were simply hurt by life, but soon they chose to keep hurting others. It's why children of divorced or abusive or alcoholic parents also become those very things, because they couldn't cut the cycle. I don't mean to showcase them as a "warning." I still believe that they could turn themselves around.

It could be that nothing ever changes around you for the better. We could be stuck in a lifelong struggle where the storm clouds never leave. We are captives to this present darkness. **But when it seems you have zero options, you still have one.** *You can still choose who you will become.*

You're already choosing. You're already calling out. The call itself is a good thing, for an unbreakable peace. But to obtain this anywhere else is to steal from others what they cannot give us. It's to steal from yourself what is not in you.

It seems God is trying to thwart in you the very thing that He knows can kill us: that our hurt can lead us to hurtful things.

It would only make sense that Jeremiah says, *Call out to Him.*

He doesn't want us to call on anything else. Even if we hate God in our lowest moment of pain: the bare minimum is that God would not want you to turn to lesser things, because they will make you a lesser version of you.

With Every Pitiful Fiber in My Fallen Being: I Call Out

We see what *not* to call out to. What about where to call?

The hard part is that when you decide not to call on other things, suddenly you're inside the pain. It's all there. You can't do anything to hide it anymore. It seems like a terrible idea.

One of the toughest things about excruciating pain is that it's embarrassing. There's a humiliating stench of astonishment that *this is happening to me.* It's *malheur,* or a pain about your pain. If you live with it long enough, you'll begin to identify yourself by your hurt, as if this is your only value. It's understandable, because it takes up so much space in your mind. It's no wonder why we're tempted to run to everything else.

The pain is blinding. But — blinding ourselves to the pain is even worse. In doing so, we erase ourselves down to the bottom.

So then: Calling out to Him is *remembering who you are.*

Remembering where you come from.

Remembering what you were made for.

Remembering that you are not your pain.

Most of all, *remembering who He is.*

This will look different for everyone. It could mean taking a long drive to the shoreline. It could mean standing over the sea in total silence. It could mean opening your Bible to Isaiah 40 or Psalm 23. It means asking a friend to hot chocolate and hearing you out. It means actively seeking encouragement and community, because 1 John 4:12 says, *"No one has ever seen God; but if we love one another, God lives in us and his love is made complete in us."* It means journaling, or busting out your guitar, or crying for a long time, or having an intense conversation with yourself. It means finding a need and serving that need. It means finding an older brother or sister and asking for wisdom on what to do next. It means dressing your Sunday best and singing at church at the top of your lungs, in hot tears and laughter.

A lot of this might feel rote and mechanical. You might not feel like doing any of it, and I don't mean to add another burden on your hurt.

I just know that for a moment, when I can trace the sunbeam back to the sun, I remember who I am. It doesn't make me instantly whole. It doesn't solve things today. It's often just a brief glimpse. But when I return to the heart who made me, I momentarily find something stronger than my pain. It is stronger than everything else that calls my name.

This is a difficult thing to do. It's not merely psychological re-arrangement, because it requires getting up. It requires tapping into a very fine frequency, which is there for a flash and gone. But it's there.

You might have even been on the other side of this and helped someone else remember. Maybe you took someone to lunch and listened to them without interruption for an hour. You made actual eye-to-eye contact, and you never knew, but you changed the course of that person's day from driving off a cliff. You randomly volunteered. You wrote a thank you note. You picked up a call from a distant friend. You wrestled with someone's questions, maybe not even fully paying attention, but you stayed with it to the end.

You didn't know, but you were part of the frequency.

Once in a while, God breaks in. He reminds us of beauty. The pain doesn't stop, but there's a joy in the middle of it, just loud enough to remember.

We can break in, too.

You can pray. You can sing. You can seek others. You can visit home in His Word.

It is painful, sloppy, and scary. It's not easy to turn our internal axis to Him, especially in hard times. But by slow, stumbling degrees, I can breathe Him in — and He is the only air that fills these crumpled lungs.

I remember: we're not home yet.

"I have a notion that what seem our worst prayers may really be, in God's eyes, our best. Those, I mean, which are least supported by devotional feeling and contend with the greatest disinclination. For these, perhaps, being nearly all will, come from a deeper level than feeling. In feeling there is so much that is really not ours — so much that comes from weather and health or from the last book read. One thing seems certain. It is no good angling for the rich moments. God sometimes seems to speak to us most intimately when he catches us, as it were, off our guard."[33]

"He works on us in all sorts of ways: not only through what we think our 'religious life.' He works through Nature, through our own bodies, through books, sometimes through experiences which seem (at the time) anti-Christian ... [He is] really coming and interfering with your very self; killing the old natural self in you and replacing it with the kind of self He has. At first, only for moments. Then for longer periods, Finally, if all goes well, turning you permanently into a different sort of thing; into a new little Christ, a being which, in its own small way, has the same kind of life as God; which shares in His power, joy, knowledge and eternity."[34]

— C.S. Lewis

On Hold: Holding On To Holding On: Hold On

The amazing thing is that God does rescue the Israelites by ending the Babylonian Captivity. They get the best outcome.

God already promised this final liberation in Jeremiah 29:14, which says, *"I will be found by you," declares the LORD, "and will bring you back from captivity. I will gather you from all the nations and places where I have banished you," declares the LORD.*

This happened. Historians wrote that the Captivity ended in 539 BC.

This means it took about *seventy years*. Most of the original Israelites would've been long dead before freedom, and the children who went free would've been molded by the pagan culture.

---

[33] C.S. Lewis, *Letters to Malcolm: Chiefly on Prayer* (FL: Harcourt, 1963, 1992) p. 116
[34] C.S. Lewis, *Mere Christianity* (NY: HarperCollins, 1952, 1980) p. 190-191

No one knew when or how, but their captivity would end, and it did.

If we put all these verses together, then we discover Jeremiah was telling his fellow Israelites: *Life is hard right now, but God will come through for us. Until then, don't call on anything else. You'll want to, but nothing else will come through for you. Call on Him alone.*

I'll make it more simple.

1) The Context: Life is hard.

2) The Problem: You'll want to escape.

3) The Promise: God has written the ending, but it could be a while until we get there.

4) The Plan: In the waiting, His plan is: *Call on Him.*

5) The Conclusion: Life is hard — but He is with you.

We don't know why the Israelites were enslaved in Babylon for seventy years. We don't know why the Israelites were enslaved in Egypt for four-hundred years.

But we *do* know that pain is inevitable. Life is hard. It will look hopeless.

I want you to know that we'll still have a hard time hearing the Bible on Sunday mornings when our life has broken into a million pieces. It doesn't *feel* like God is listening sometimes. For as much as we've traveled through these verses together, I know it won't always be enough to hold you up. When life is on hold, it's hard to hold on.

I get emails every week that break my heart every time: a woman tells me her husband, also a pastor, is addicted to crack and gambling and prostitutes, and she's afraid to divorce him because it could ruin all the good in their church. A daughter tells me her parents have disowned her because of her faith, her school, her boyfriend. A dear brother tells me he has a disease that causes constant pain in his skin and he wants to end it every second. A dear sister tells me she cannot go an hour without thinking about self-harm and her self-image.

They're captives. I hurt for them, all the time. Maybe it's obvious to you and me what the answer should be: but when you're there, you are trapped at every turn.

I don't know why some of us have to wait for seven weeks or seven months or seventy years. I don't know why some of us live with lifelong terminal issues that will never resolve. I can't tell you why some of us are still in captivity.

I don't know if it's enough for my friend Grace.

When I'm in that awful place, it's downright painful to call out to God. I want to blame Him instead. It feels like I'm making contact with the very person who threw me in this pit. It's counter-intuitive. It makes my stomach turn.

But I don't know where else I would go. It's the only place I can find the peace I've been chasing. Not answers, but rest. Even for one more breath.

Before we get to the outcome: I believe we have a God who hears us in the worst moments of our journey, with strength for the very next step.

By the tiniest shred of faith, you can bring all the flailing responses from your pain to God Himself. Our exposed, raw nerve brings about the worst in us — but we wrestle with it, measure it, fight it, navigate the mess inside, each and every day. And this is the dark part of us that God can shape, re-shape, and wholly heal. It's not easy. I don't mean to make it sound pretty.

It's hard to endure here, but it's harder *not* to. Life will hurt anyway, whether you sit down or move forward. We will bleed anyway, and healing hurts even worse, because we must do the hard work of walking in our wounds. **But I would rather hurt by healing than hurt by choosing to wallow in what happened to me.** I would rather hurt standing up than sitting down. I would rather hurt looking up than looking away. God knows that the best way to look forward is to look up. The only way to de-internalize our pain is to release it in the safest place possible.

My friend Grace really believes it, you know. She doesn't know the *why* stuff, but she knows the *what* and the *how*. When there are no options, she still has the one, and nothing can take that from her. It's enough for today, and maybe that's enough for always.

We don't know how this will end.

We can only choose who we'll be when we get there.

"We are not necessarily doubting that God will do the best for us; we are wondering how painful the best will turn out to be."[35]
— C.S. Lewis

---

[35] C.S. Lewis, Warnie Lewis, *Letters of C.S. Lewis* (NY: Harcourt, 1966) p. 256

I was seven years old when I got in my first street fight in the only tenements that my parents — struggling poor Koreans they were — could afford. I had fought a much older single mother and lost. To my credit, she started it. At twelve years old, I decided I was an atheist. At fourteen, my parents divorced, as if to confirm that God couldn't exist. At sixteen, I had my first drop of an ensuing ocean of alcohol. That same year, I went to what they called a "Gentleman's Club" and stumbled upon a terrible addiction. By nineteen, I had lost my college scholarship and dropped out with a 0.9 GPA. By twenty-two, I had swallowed a bottle of pills over the girl I was living with, who had cheated on me twice. I spent time in what they call a "mental institution," which was perhaps an improvement over the Gentleman's Club.

I understand these problems do not compare to those of the world over: but the contrast was that I hardly felt anything. I was following the latest, loudest emotion, just the exit ramps to the bigger neon sign. And soon I was staring into the mouth of a senseless life with little purpose and no meaning — and it was all rather hilarious.

In my apprehension towards all-things-God, I would stay up until three in the morning watching the ceiling fan, knowing there was more to life than the empty vacuum of sweaty drunk faces and the smear of red-and-blue cop car lights. At some point in college I was certain that God was at least a real being, if only because I had looked into the face of nothingness and knew that no one could possibly sustain a life in that direction. But I didn't want there to be a God, not with a capital G. It was horrifying to think so. It was crazy to think I couldn't call my own shots and that I was somehow not the main character of my own existence.

I went to church anyway. Quite faithfully, too. I got caught up in the music, the messages, the social fervor, that moment after the sermon in the lobby when no one talks about the sermon. I started bringing my friends by the dozens because I was good at that sort of thing. And somewhere along the line, almost imperceptibly by degrees, I started hearing the messages. I really started listening. I heard about a God who loves us and became one of us and died for us and defeated death and invited us into the best relationship there is. Not a God who gives us everything we want, because that would be no better than Santa Claus with a pager. But a glorious, grand, dynamic, pulsating God, who was writing this incredible drama with His Son at the apex of history and letting us all in. Even letting me in. Almost by accident, to my growing disdain, I was feeling alive for the first time.

A few years in, I went to this huge conference. There were probably 10,000 people. I was both excited and uneasy because it rubbed against my dislike for the institutional manufactured hype of religious emotionalism, but then it was quite a sight to see so many Christians singing and praying and even taking notes during the sermon. The praise leader, Matt, was apparently famous and he shared his testimony. He said when he was just a kid, he had been molested by his uncle, and in that same bed, Matt had written worship songs.

I couldn't comprehend this sort of resilience. That sort of hurt would've turned me off God forever. And I came around to thinking that my hatred against faith was merely a conditioned childish rebellion against Santa Claus and not the real God, because my childhood was all kinds of unfair and screwed up and wrong. I had been shaking a fist at a phantom of my own trauma, wrought by a misconception of "God" who I could blame any time I didn't get what I wanted. I thought my objections were intellectual and foolproof and full of scientific defense, but really I was just regurgitating the same anger that the human race had displaced from their disappointing parents onto the easy target of a keychain-pager-God.

There was suddenly the invasive uncomfortable idea that perhaps God was real and He had a name and He actually wanted to know me — and

He didn't wave a wand to make everything easier, but He did promise Himself inside the furnace of our broken chaotic mess.

Predictably enough, I began to cry. I couldn't stop. I was with my friend and he began to cry too. We were both really embarrassed but we prayed for each other, and I think I heard God say, "You have a story to share."

At the end of 2007, I applied for my seminary. Despite my really weird school record, they graciously accepted. It turns out that ministry is not a picnic, at all. No one told me how hard it would really be. But as I took those first baby steps into loving the unloved, I found that this was the path I never knew I wanted but had always been made for. I began to believe God made me to share a story: namely, His. I went feet first into the places where no one else would go, to wretched doubters and picketing haters and the impoverished and ostracized and fatherless, and there I would tell them about grace and a mission and a final home, and that this earth was not it. I embraced the calling to give away my life so that others may see life.

I'm not saying that you need to be a pastor. I'm not saying that you need a wild story to be "useful." I'm not saying there's a binary choice between the world and your soul. I'm not saying I'm better than anyone else.

I just know what God can do through people like me, and like you.

I'm still not sure that God uses such pain to make us stronger.

But I believe He can make us stronger than the pain.

This is our testimony.

When you call out to Him: He has been calling to you all along.

— J.S.

"People often think of Christian morality as a kind of bargain in which God says, 'If you keep a lot of rules I'll reward you, and if you don't I'll do the other thing.' I do not think that is the best way of looking at it. I would much rather say that every time you make a choice you are turning the central part of you, the part of you that chooses, into something a little different from what it was before. And taking your life as a whole, with all your innumerable choices, all your life long you are slowly turning this central thing either into a heavenly creature or into a hellish creature: either into a creature that is in harmony with God, and with other creatures, and with itself, or else into one that is in a state of war and hatred with God, and with its fellow-creatures, and with itself.

"To be the one kind of creature is heaven: that is, it is joy and peace and knowledge and power. To be the other means madness, horror, idiocy, rage, impotence, and eternal loneliness. Each of us at each moment is progressing to the one state or the other.

"... If we let Him—for we can prevent Him, if we choose—He will make the feeblest and filthiest of us into a god or goddess, a dazzling, radiant, immortal creature, pulsating all through with such energy and joy and wisdom and love as we cannot now imagine, a bright stainless mirror which reflects back to God perfectly (though, of course, on a smaller scale) His own boundless power and delight and goodness. The process will be long and in parts very painful; but that is what we are in for. Nothing less. He meant what He said."[36]

— C.S. Lewis

[36] C.S. Lewis, *Mere Christianity* ((NY: HarperCollins, 1952, 1980) p.93, 207

THE PROBLEM WITH GOLIATH:

David's stones will solve your debt and marriage crisis

[INTERLUDE 2]

Interlude 2
The Problem With Goliath: David's Stones Will Solve Your Debt and Marriage Crisis

When You Miss All Five Stones: Crushed Dreams and Gripping The Death-Grip

One of the deepest pains in life is losing a dream you had of the future: but even worse is the frenzy to get it back. We can get so obsessed with a particular idea of the future that we find it impossible to let go.

Preachers like me will reinforce this by telling you that failures are just obstacles. You've heard this sermon before.

"What's your Goliath? Bad finances? Failed marriage? Poor health? You can overcome your giant! You can raise that Lazarus to life! You can lead like Nehemiah and split your sea like Moses! Be like Ruth and get your Boaz!"

Besides the mishandling of Scripture, it also introduces another burden. Matt Chandler asks the question:

"What happens when your stone misses? What happens when you throw all five stones and all five stones miss? What happens when with all your effort and all your might and all your power, you don't slay the giant?"[37]

---

[37] Matt Chandler, "David, Goliath, & The Gospel." http://vimeo.com/34692625

The thing is, many of us have already missed.

Many of us walk into church already beat up by the consequences of our choices.

We've had our dreams crushed by Goliath.

Then you're told you just need to try harder, chase longer, do more. It only kicks you while you're down.

Using a moral ideal doesn't help your reality. David and Nehemiah and Ruth had many great qualities, but they were people, just like you and me. They had the same problems. They failed just as often. Not even David could be like David. Using biblical figures as an "example" is exhausting. If I exhort you to "Be like Paul" or "Be like Jesus," it's an unsustainable standard that will strangle you into moral fatigue.

The truth is that if you live long enough, you end up walking in the shattered remains of an old dream. You messed it up the one time and now your family is in ruins. You went for that one relationship, the one night, the one invite, that one weekend, and then it was *too late*. Whether it was you or the people around you: your life has a clear splice between *before* and *after*. At some point, there was no going back, and now you're wading through the wreckage.

At first you had a death-grip on your past: but now you have a death-grip on your death-grip. Maybe no one told you that we fail, we move on, and that's life.

You can fail without being a failure.

Sometimes, life just doesn't work out. It's not because you didn't try hard enough. It's not because you made the worst possible choice. It has nothing to do with your character or ability.

It just didn't work out.

You're Missing Out On God's Will: The Late Night Regret Twitch

When it doesn't work out, many of us believe we've fallen into a mediocre Plan B.

It bothers us pretty bad. The regrets.

You've had the Late-Night Regret Twitch: to mourn over why we couldn't have just done better. There are defining moments in the past where we think, "I should've went to that city. I should've gotten that job. I never should've dated her. I wish I could un-meet him."

My dear friend: If you've really messed it up, I don't believe you can "fall off" God's Will. I don't believe that God's Will could be a fixed straight line. I don't think God ever says, "Well, you fell off the track so good luck in the ditch for the rest of your life."

Many earnest Christians assume that *this* relationship or *this* job or *this* house is the one that God really has for them, so they invest their entire heart into these things. But at any moment, our idea of the future can be upturned. We see it happen all the time. Did that mean God had it coming for them? Does that mean they're now out of line with God's Will and they need to claw for their dream again?

This is crucial because there will be appropriate times to let something go.

I don't believe it's "God's Will" for you to keep one picture of your life by the skin of your teeth. I would never endorse that you can change your mind when you feel like it, nor endorse that you can divorce when it gets hard, nor run out when you're uncomfortable. No one should ever use "God's Will" as a trump-card to burn bridges. We're all called to persevere, to stay determined, to finish strong. But there will be times when you need to correct your entire course, and it's okay to start over. It's unfair to use "God's Will" as an excuse to quit, but also unfair to use it as an iron grip to endure past an expiration date. Both of these are equally dangerous errors.

When I read Scripture, I see that most of the biblical characters had to change choices on the fly. They would run into a dead end, back up, and start again. They spent years in circles. Sometimes God would reveal what to do next; other times they would just pack up and start walking. Their lives were flexible. They didn't have *one specific dream.* They did mess up, a lot. I'm sure they had tons of Late-Night Regret Twitching. I'm sure, like us, they often thought, "It's too late for me." *But in hindsight, the very interruptions and unforeseen circumstances in their lives were part of God's Plan A.* Every wrinkle in their story was a new doorway. And God's Will, in the end, wasn't so much about what they were doing, but the *kind of person* they were becoming. The destination was important, but the journey was the pulse that beat their hearts.

Sure, you'll miss second chances and opportunities in your time here on earth. Yes, I believe God's commands are for your good, and if you run against them, you won't have a good time. On a long enough timeline, you'll make some irreversible regrets and some undoable choices.

The thing is: *You can't really make up for lost time.* If you try to compensate for what's behind you, you won't be able to look ahead. It's like starting a race from negative two laps. This is a losing game, and the only way to win is to admit loss and start over.

When I first learned how to drive, I had a bad habit of looking in the rearview mirror all the time. My dad would tell me: *Don't worry about the car behind you. That's their job. You look straight ahead.* Sounds like something Jesus said: *Don't worry about tomorrow, for tomorrow will worry about itself.*

I'm not telling you to never look in the rearview. I'm saying: **We can't live our lives looking both forward and backward at the same time.**

It will not be easy. But it won't be any easier if you keep looking over your shoulder.

> *"Calling has this weight that somehow we think that your calling is fixed. That your calling is this line that you've finally found and now you're on that track and that's what you're gonna do forever and maybe that the case. But I feel like calling has much more to do with the moment that you're in."*[38]
> — Jon Foreman

The Pressure To Be Great and Radical and Missional and Purposeful: Our Hollywood Craze To Live An Epic Life

At times the church culture will give us audacious, bombastic, grandiose visions of *radical purpose.* Instead of being like David, we're going all the way to *Be-Like-Jesus.*

---

[38] http://www.relevantmagazine.com/culture/music/choosing-believe-jon-foreman

To be truthful, I think these are great. I think the church is called to be as outlandish as possible for the best reasons. In 2012, I gave away half my salary to charity to fight human trafficking.[39] I don't say that to brag; it was insanely difficult and I wanted to quit many times. But if churches around the world combined their assets this very second, we could probably eliminate poverty and preventable diseases in our lifetime.

I'm on board with big visions. But — a "big vision" is usually one more moral shackle in church-world. In a culture of David-Vs-Goliath, we've raised the bar so high that we think we're worthless unless we're doing "great things for God." It only causes more pain and guilt.

I was talking with a friend the other day who felt like he was missing out on God's Great Plan. I asked him what he meant. He said, "I was always told I would do something great with my life. That God could do great things through me." He's currently studying in one of the best law schools in the world to be a lawyer and has already worked for multiple law firms around the world.

I wondered, *Isn't God already doing great things through you?*

This painful pressure to be "great" is an impossible threshold. I don't believe we all need to start a non-profit or give up our salary or build an orphanage. We're not all called to be singers and actors and authors, as if that's the only acceptable standard. It's great to do those things. But it's just as great to love

---

[39] Eugene Cho, *Overrated* (CO: David C. Cook, 2014) pp. 183-185
http://eugenecho.com/2012/11/26/an-inspiring-story-of-courage-and-generosity-youth-pastor-donates-half-of-his-salary-to-fight-human-trafficking/
http://jspark3000.tumblr.com/post/66676427478/why-did-i-donate-half-my-salary

people where you are. It's just as great to change diapers, hand out bulletins, and sweep the hallway.

The verses that say we must "become like Jesus" don't necessarily mean we become monks and fast from everything and give away all our stuff. That's all very possible, but sometimes it's a cop-out. When we "share in Jesus's suffering,"[40] all these verses point to love for one another. It's to pay the cost of love. What I mean is, *real love will always cost you something, because it demands you give away a part of yourself.* That sort of costly love is called grace. **Grace is the love that hurts.** Real love always suffers. The moment you enter into someone's mess, it's no longer a cute workshop of willing people who will do as you say. Everyone loves the idea of love until it comes to unlovable people. It requires a staying power, a perseverance that isn't natural to our fickle feet. It's not the huge Hollywood dream we so often preach about.

This could still mean becoming a missionary, but it also validates the daily grind of persevering with your family, your church, your neighborhood.

Sometimes, taking down Goliath happens gradually, limb by limb, without a big stage.

> *"Even if it falls your lot to be a street sweeper, go on out and sweep streets like Michelangelo painted pictures; sweep streets like Handel and Beethoven composed music; sweep streets like Shakespeare wrote poetry; sweep streets so well that all the host of heaven and earth will have to pause and say, 'Here lived a great street sweeper who swept his job well.'*

---

[40] Philippians 3:10, Colossians 1:24

"If you can't be a highway, just be a trail. If you can't be the sun, be a star. It isn't by size that you win or fail. Be the best of whatever you are. And when you do this, when you do this, you've mastered the length of life."[41]
— Dr. Martin Luther King, Jr.

The Voice of Self-Condemnation: Breaking The Perpetual Loop of the Small Town Time-Stamp

I still do want you to reach for your goals. I know how difficult this can be in a small town when others around you define you by your past. It seems like no one wants to give you a chance. If you've grown up in the same town long enough — everyone assumes you're the same person you always were, and they can't see past the past version of you.

I've been in the same city for a long time and I've done many awful things. There are days I keep imagining what other people are saying about me. I imagine a room full of them laughing at me, shaking their heads saying, "I always knew something was wrong with him." It keeps me up at night. I wake up to it in the mirror. I mentally argue with them until I've finally proven I'm not who I used to be. I'll spend hours inside my own head explaining my side of the story and why you need to know I'm not a bad guy and that I'm sorry for the person I was before. Really. Hours. I can't seem to do a single good thing without the throttling voice of condemnation cutting into my head. It

---

[41] Martin Luther King, Jr., "The Three Dimensions of a Complete Life." Preached at Friendship Baptist Church. February 28th, 1960

squeezes the value of any good I could do. Even when I win the argument in my angry fantasies, I'm not at peace; I'm more mad than when I started.

You're not the good guy you pretend to be.

I know who you really are.

I know what you're about.

You're not fooling anyone.

Actual things people have said to me:

"You're just ugly."

"I've lost all respect for you."

"You're beyond repair."

"All this God-stuff can't change you."

"Obviously you hate children."

"You're just a nobody pastor. You'll never make it."

I get into a mental shut-down, a constant tortured paralysis, not allowing myself any joy for too long, because I feel this is a righteous punishment. Sometimes I write a secret arrow aimed at those people and I hope the next time they see me they're so, so sorry.

Life can feel like a constant game of compensation and always apologizing for the past and there's this paranoia that I'm always doing something wrong, that life will pay me back, that others will misinterpret me no matter what I do.

Are we all doomed to our former selves, time-stamped to who we used to be? Will this loop of second-guessing and self-condemning never end?

Sometimes I think the remedy is to assume that everyone else is Goliath.

Every hater is a Pharisee. They're the "enemy." They're all just trolls. It's the language of the infidel: I make it about *Me* versus *Them*.

But they are not Goliath.

I am not David.

I've found that *the very same people who I thought were judging me also felt like they were being judged by others.* We share the same insecurity. We live with the same dead dreams. We have the same voice of self-condemnation.

Or as Dietrich Bonhoeffer says,

"We must learn to regard people less in the light of what they do or omit to do, and more in the light of what they suffer."[42]

If we were to sit down for an hour over coffee, we would understand a bit more. That we have the same hopes, dreams, passions, and ambitions. That we are not so different. That we've both failed. We both have a past. That we love children, love dogs, love good movies, laugh at viral videos, and weep at tragic headlines. That we share fears, addictions, complexes, and worries. You'd certainly see horrible things in me, but perhaps you'd feel love instead of judgment. You'd see we're both multi-dimensional people who fight the same battles with our multiple split selves, and that you and I are not stock archetypes from a backyard Disney vault. We are real, gritty, imperfect: just people.

Maybe we could see we don't always get it right, and that our failures should not give us a weaponized filter to suffocate everything we do.

---

[42] Dietrich Bonhoeffer, *Letters and Papers from Prison* (NY, Touchstone, 1953, 1971) p. 10

A New Dream:
Crazy Hard

I did a short-term mission trip for a prison ministry in Chicago and I met a guy named Kim. Kim had been in and out of jail for burglary. At one point, he had robbed over twenty houses in two weeks. He was addicted to cocaine, but he was just as addicted to robbing houses. Kim said, "I would get high, and then I would really get high."

One night he was robbing a place and it happened it be the home of a police officer. They both showed up in the hall at the same time: robber, meet policeman. They paused for about a full five seconds, and then the police officer ran for his gun. Kim jumped out a window. The officer managed to fire a few shots, and one of them hit Kim in the ribs.

Kim walked a few miles to the nearest hospital. They placed him under arrest. He quit snorting coke; he quit snorting houses.

I was expecting some miraculous ending. But he said, "Life is still crazy hard. Just hard."

He couldn't get a job anywhere and his girlfriend was still in and out of jail. Cocaine constantly whispered his name; every house he saw was a treasure chest waiting to be busted open. He eventually got a job at a graveyard, working night shifts, but he was scared all the time because it was full of dead people. Life was a fight, every single day, and he couldn't gloss that over.

He told me, "They say that you need to hit rock bottom in order to quit the old life. Boy, *ain't no rock bottom*. It keeps going down and down, hitting the wall the whole way down. You can go as low as you want. Ain't nobody tell you that until you falling."

Then he said, "My girlfriend is about to finish her time. Got her job lined up. We're getting married. I'm okay, you know. Ain't the dream I wanted, but thank God, I still got one."

Meanwhile, Start

My friend: I know you might have had a picture of how you wanted your life to be, but some uncontrollable tragedy swept it away.

We all have a certain picture of how we want our lives to be, and sometimes it gets ripped from our grip and smashed to pieces. Our dreams can get crushed in an instant, in the most horrible ways, with irreversible results.

We might be living in a life right now that doesn't feel like it's ours, you and I. We might be in a different place than we had hoped for. Today could be different than you had imagined and planned a year ago. Your heart will pull for another chance, another door, another world.

We wake up in a daze, wondering how things changed so fast.

We wait, hoping it'll go back to the way it was.

The three hardest words to live with are often: *In the meantime.*

Yet — in the meantime is the whole thing. We'll always think the grass is greener somewhere else. But as Eugene Cho says, *"If you ever feel like the grass is greener on the other side, that's the Holy Spirit telling you to water your damn grass."*[43]

If you're waiting for your "real life" to start, after graduation or when you're married or when you get to the big city, you'll stay in a holding pattern. The time will pass anyway. The tide doesn't wait.

So I hope you'll consider starting in the meanwhile.

When a dream dies, it dies. We can mourn. We can pound our chest. We can bleed. And at some point, we must let go and not linger. You can open your hands to another dream. **I hope you find this new dream.** I hope you don't try to revive something that's dead.

You can get over what's over, because you're not over yet.

When the ten count is over: you can count to eleven.

What comes next will not be what you had envisioned. It might be better or it might be worse. I hope you will keep dreaming anyway. I hope you will consider God can do a new thing.

You are free to pursue something new.

"You must ask for God's help. Even when you have done so, it may seem to you for a long time that no help, or less help than you need, is being given. Never mind. After each failure, ask forgiveness, pick yourself up, and try again. Very often what God first helps us towards is not the virtue itself but just this power of always trying again."[44]

— C.S. Lewis

---

[43] Eugene Cho, "The Most Over-Rated Generation."Preached at Catalyst 2011. October 5th, 2011

[44] C.S. Lewis, *Mere Christianity* (NY: HarperCollins, 1952, 1980) p. 102

Andy Versus Shawshank:
Redeeming The Meanwhile

The movie *Shawshank Redemption,* at its very core, is about a man who does his best in a bad situation. He's all about *the meanwhile.* The movie works because we like Andy Dufresne. He's a modern day Joseph, falsely accused of a crime and thrown into prison, but never quite imprisoned. Andy stays hopeful in a broken system that does not allow for hopeful men like him.

There are common beats for this sort of story: a small victory, a large defeat, another small victory, another crippling defeat. The episodic nature gives it almost a biblical sense of time, each part a microcosm of these men's lives punctuated by a continuing narrative of good versus evil. Andy is unflappable, persistent, almost maddening in his strive to better things around him. He succeeds at much of it. But just as it begins to feel too easy, hope is struck down. Andy is deflated over and over again. He is nearly strangled of his spirits. Of course, he is never quite destroyed.

In one of the best scenes, Andy plays music over a loudspeaker for the entire prison. The men are mesmerized: in their eyes you can see another lifetime before this whole mess. When Andy finishes his punishment of solitary confinement — something all the prisoners fear — he remarks, "Easiest time I ever did." At moments like these he has a bemused smile, like he got away with something wonderful. We cheer for him.

Most of the prisoners plead they're innocent. They've rationalized their crimes. They avoid the cliché of bad men with golden hearts; most of the men are hardened criminals that belong in Shawshank. The movie avoids a fairytale environment where everyone wants to change, and this is true of tired people who are worn down by their unwise choices. Andy is like a chemical shock in the cesspool. Not everyone welcomes this because they prefer to remain hopeless. We'd all like to say that evil has won and God is dead. It's easier.

There are other tiny stories in the movie, some hopeful and some heartbreaking, and they all serve the same theme: that life is worth living in the darkest of times because it's worth living at all. Andy's friend Red, a man who supplies his fellow prisoners with cigarettes and other contraband, is at odds with Andy's wide-eyed intensity. "Hope is a dangerous thing," Red says. "Hope can drive a man insane." Several times I felt Red was right. We sense by the end that Andy wants to give up, too.

While the prison itself is an enemy of its own, we meet Warden Norton, one of the movie villain greats. His suit, his haircut, his glasses, his speech: all of these are indicators that he is in for a glorious downfall. Think Satan in the final chapters of Revelation. I've never wanted to so badly reach into a television screen and slap a fictional villain. This is Batman's Joker, Superman's Luthor, Spiderman's puberty. But the warden has all the power; Andy only has his brains and that indomitable heart. We keep cheering.

A film like *Shawshank Redemption* reminds us that in spite of evil's desperate hold over humanity, it's fleeting. We'd like to think that good guys win by default because they're good. We know from the news this isn't true. Sometimes evil wins the day because it doesn't play fair. But Andy is the passionate reservoir of the good fight in all of us. Andy fights his pain by fighting pain in the world. He keeps dreaming by giving dreams to others. He refuses the status quo. He pays attention to those around him. He brings healing, even to the villains. He conquers Goliath over a lifetime.

It takes that long. We will miss, we will lose, we will fall down — but these setbacks don't get to say who we are. When it doesn't work out, you and I can still work. There's no such thing as fighting empty so long as you're still fighting. True victory happens the moment after you're defeated, when you decide to get up again. It happens when you take hold of the hand extended from heaven, one bloody palm to another.

Therefore we do not lose heart.
Though outwardly we are wasting away,
yet inwardly we are being renewed day by day.
For our light and momentary troubles are achieving for us
an eternal glory that far outweighs them all.
So we fix our eyes not on what is seen,
but on what is unseen.
For what is seen is temporary,
but what is unseen is eternal.
— 2 Corinthians 4:16-18

You might have failed somewhere else, completely fallen on your face in a mushroom cloud you caused, and it haunts you now as you enter the next season of life. But as you receive a second chance in your new opportunities: give yourself a chance too. Please don't allow former hurts to become a filter through which you approach others. Please don't instantly assume that similar behaviors and attitudes from your last situation can be accusations against the new one. Approach each decision with a fresh set of eyes, free of suspicion and paranoia, but most of all, without judging yourself by the weight of what happened before.

It's easy to pass on the pain we received in a never-ending vicious cycle — but we can choose in our new seasons to cut that loop, to interrupt our old patterns with new life, to absorb the hurt with grace, to allow our wounds to heal into a strength we could not have previously known. We could re-build and re-create. It's how we move forward. It's how we got the second chance at all: because someone risked that chance on us first.

— J.S.

*We get glimpses of **"God's Plan."***

Those glorious moments when it does work out.

We look back and see how it all fell into place.

We see the barest hints of a Rube Goldberg machine, unwinding, unfolding.

We see the close calls, the tiny little inches where each interlocking piece came together.

It is like a prism in reverse, pulling all the strands of unrelated colors into a shaft of white light, piercing the dark — and for a moment, I can truly believe that God creates sense out of the senseless.

It's not like this all the time. I don't always get the Plan. It is hard to trust Him.

But sometimes, I see. And it is harder not to trust God for the things I have seen.

Ravi Zacharias tells the story of a Vietnamese man, Hien Pham, an interpreter imprisoned by the Viet Cong, held captive during the Vietnam War.[45]

In Dr. Ravi's own words:

> My phone rang. I was in Vancouver speaking and the phone rang at 11:00 p.m. The man said, "Brother Ravi." There's only one person who called me with that intonation that way. I said, "Hien, is that you?" he said, "Yes." I said, "Oh my word! Where are you?" He said, "California." I said, "What are you doing here?" He said, "Have you got a few minutes?" I said, "Yes."
>
> He said, "After Vietnam fell, I was imprisoned by the Viet Cong because I'd worked with the Americans, worked with people like you. They put me behind bars, they took away all

---

[45] http://rzim.org/just-thinking/national-day-of-prayer-address

English from me, took away my Bible from me, tried to knock faith out of me. I was only allowed to read Marx and Engels in French and Vietnamese. After about a year in there, so worn out, I said, 'Maybe you don't exist, God. I'm giving up all hope. I don't believe in you. Tomorrow when I wake up, I'm not going to pray.'"

That morning, he was assigned to clean the latrines. He said, "Brother Ravi, it's the dirtiest place on earth you'd want to be. I bound a handkerchief around my mouth cleaning the wet floor, and I saw a little bin with dirty pieces of paper, with human excrement in it. But something told me as I looked there, there was one paper, a piece of paper with English." He said, "I hadn't read English for so long. I washed it off, put it in my hip pocket, waited for everybody to go to bed, to sleep. Lights were out.

I took out my flashlight under my mosquito net. I flashed it. On the right hand corner it said, Romans chapter 8." He said, "I started reading and cried. 'Oh, my dear Lord, you didn't leave me one day without you.' 'For all things work together for good to them that love God; to those that are called according to his purpose. For who shall separate us from the love of Christ? Neither things present, nor things to come, nor life nor death.'"

Hien said, "Next morning I went back to the commanding officer. I said, 'Do you mind if I clean the latrines again today?'" He went there every day. He found another page from the New Testament. The commanding officer had been given a Bible a long time ago. He was tearing out a page every day using it as toilet paper. Hien was washing it and using it for his devotions every day.

I said, "Where are you now?" He said, "I'm at Berkeley doing my business degree." I said, "I can't believe this, Hien." He said, "I'm in America."

I said, "How did that happen?" He said, "I was released and I built a boat with 52 others. Four days before my release, before our escape, four Viet Cong came armed to the teeth and grabbed me and said, 'Are you trying to escape?' I lied and said, 'No.' They said, 'Are you telling us the truth?'" He said, "Yes."

They let him go. He got on his knees, and said, "God, I lied. I'm running my own life. I lied. If you really want me to tell them the truth, let them come back again." He said, "I sincerely hoped that prayer would never be answered. Hours before we left, the four of them came with their machine guns, grabbed me by the collar, rammed me against the wall. 'You're lying, aren't you?'"

Hien said, "Yes, I'm escaping with 52 others. Are you going to imprison me again?" They said, "No. we want to go with you.'"

"Brother Ravi, if it weren't for them we would never have made it. They knew how to navigate the ocean on that boat, get us safely to Thailand. I was then listed as a United Nations refugee. I'm here in America now doing my business degree."

He runs a financial planning company now in California. He came and visited us, wanted me to officiate at his wedding, and he looked at my kids and said, "Don't ever think God is far away from you. That intimate relationship is the greatest thrill of anyone's life, for He seeks such to have fellowship with Him."

"For my thoughts are not your thoughts,
neither are your ways my ways,"
declares the LORD.
"As the heavens are higher than the earth,
so are my ways higher than your ways
and my thoughts than your thoughts.
As the rain and the snow come down from heaven,
 and do not return to it without watering the earth
and making it bud and flourish,
so that it yields seed for the sower and bread for the eater,
so is my word that goes out from my mouth:
It will not return to me empty,
but will accomplish what I desire
and achieve the purpose for which I sent it."
— Isaiah 55:8-11

BROKEN BAD OR BREAKING BADLY:

Second world problems and overusing "struggle"

[CHAPTER 5]

Chapter 5

Broken Bad or Breaking Badly: Second World Problems and Overusing "Struggle"

Ashamed of My Pain: Everyday Drama

We've heard some really hard stories, and after a while, we might think, "I guess my life is not so bad." We've talked about some very awful things, about real devastation, and some of us might feel ashamed about our own pain.

If there's so much darkness in the world: does my suffering actually count?

What constitutes "real" suffering?

How do I know if it's actually struggling or just selfishness?

In a response to an article from the online magazine Cracked, a Pakistani Muslim writes about the over-use of the word "oppression."

"As a Pakistani Shi'a Muslim, you have no idea how pissed I get when people loosely use the word [oppression] in Canada. Posters for 'anti-Oppressive speech' is my favorite. I'm sorry, but speech is not, and never will be oppressive. Unless you have to flee your country of birth because you're worried that you and your loved ones will be killed for your race, religion, ethnicity, or sexual orientation ... you are not, and never will be oppressed.

You might be offended, yes. But not oppressed.

"My fellow Shi'a are being murdered senselessly in Bahrain, Iraq, Pakistan, Saudi Arabia, Nigeria and Yemen. With the rise of ISIS, I am watching the systematic genocide of our people, the Buddhists of Tibet can't even say 'Dalai' and 'Lama' in the same sentence without being thrown in a 'reeducation camp.' The Bah'ais of Iran and Saudi Arabia are being chased out en masse for their religion, the Yazidis and Christians of Iraq are being driven from their homes into the desert to die because they refuse to convert, the Muslims of Burma are getting their villages burned to the ground by angry Buddhist mobs, the people of North Korea can't even raise a finger against the Kim family without being put in front of a firing squad. So after all this, don't you dare talk about 'oppressive' language. Until you fear for your life, your safety, and your loved ones, for speaking out, you are not oppressed."[46]

This offers a jarring perspective on some of our own issues in the West, or what many have called First World Problems.[47] Albert Mohler, in his essay "Are We Raising A Nation of Wimps?" remarks that, *"Our kids are growing up to be pampered wimps who are incapable of assuming adult responsibility and have no idea how to handle the routine challenges of life."[48]*

On one hand, I absolutely agree. I believe what many call suffering today is merely over-sensitive self-pity, and it completely neglects those who are truly victims. Jerry Sittser, the professor who lost his mother, wife, and daughter in a car accident, says, *"My tragedy introduced me to a side of life that most people around the world know all too well."[49]*

---

[46] http://www.cracked.com/blog/3-controversial-words-weve-drained-meaning_p2/
[47] White Whine, a Collection of First World Problems. http://whitewhine.com/
[48] Albert Mohler, *Culture Shift* (CO: Multnomah Books, 2008, 2011) p. 70
[49] Jerry Sittser, *A Grace Disguised* (MI: Zondervan, 1995) p. 109

On the other hand, comparing problems in a competition is pointless. Jerry Sittser also says, *"I question whether experiences of such severe loss can be quantified and compared. Loss is loss, whatever the circumstances. All losses are bad, only bad in different ways. No two losses are ever the same. Each loss stands on its own and inflicts a unique kind of pain."*[50]

At times we dismiss someone's problems by pointing to a larger problem. This is called the Fallacy of Relative Privation, or *Whataboutery*. If someone says, "I have a headache," then someone responds, "What about the starving kids in Somalia?"

The problem is that it doesn't address the original problem.

It offers perspective, which we need, but doesn't offer a way out.

I want you to know that no matter the size of your problems, they're real. They might not deserve the weight of your full priority, but they're there. To simply downsize all your issues to appear humble won't help you.

If you have a credit card debt or a substance addiction, we can't compare this to a starving child in Africa or a persecuted Christian in Iraq. Of course, the latter are suffering so much more — but you're allowed to hurt, too.

You're allowed to have a bad day.

In between first world and third world problems, I believe there are **Second World Problems** that are not as bad as the suffering in the larger world, but do need your attention. They're not to be diminished, but properly estimated. They cannot be made too big, but not made too small. Issues like depression, eating disorders, bankruptcy, break-ups, loneliness, a lack of purpose, anxiety, emotional instability, and fear of the future are

---

[50] Ibid., 25

all legitimate issues. It's possible some of these could be symptoms of an entitled generation. But even if this is true, *to belittle someone for their inability to cope is still not a solution.* To tell someone, "You have no reason to have problems" is not helpful. To apologize for your petty first world problem doesn't help your problem.

"You are under no obligation to feel bad for not suffering from the same thing as someone else."[51]
— Peter D. Webb

Struggling Versus Selfishness: The Hijacking of Confrontational Honesty And The Buzzword "Struggle"

I want to be very clear that I'm not enabling, pampering, or coddling you. As much as your pain is real, we're often tempted to use relatable words like "struggle" as an excuse.

The other day, my friend tells me he's cheating on his wife. He says, "I'm really struggling."

I reply, "You're not struggling. You're cheating on your wife."

I see this sort of thing all the time. The word *struggle* allows us off the hook to continue destructive patterns. It's a subconscious green-light to "learn the hard way." It also takes away from the people who are truly struggling.

Many of us brandish this quote around with great aplomb:
"Be kind, for everyone you meet is fighting a hard battle."[52]

---

[51] Peter D. Webb. http://www.peterdwebb.com/post/104866819506/

Or as we say today, "Everyone's struggling."

I absolutely believe that everyone struggles in their own personal battle with addictions, self-condemnation, and serious deep-rooted dysfunctions — but I've seen this word abused and exaggerated for selfish complacency.

I'm beginning to suspect that this language of "the struggle" and "defeat" and "brokenness" has silently crept into permission to be downright, unashamedly selfish.

I've seen sincere strugglers really seeking help and recovery. They begin from a negative deficit because of their upbringing, their former hurts, and their uncontrollable circumstances. So then: *It actually diminishes the struggle of real hurting people if you abuse the vocabulary of "struggling broken people" for someone who's really just a self-seeking jerk.* It belittles the truly broken person who is desperate for victory over their pain.

I find it more and more difficult to believe this is true for most people, especially when there's a consistent pattern of choosing unwisely and hurting others with impunity and little care for consequences. Some of us *know* that we're deliberately sabotaging our lives. Then we smuggle in the language of "struggle" to cover for our selfish agendas.

If we water down these terms, we end up with words that mean nothing and help no one. We then enable the prideful person and we ridicule the hurting addict. We allow the wide gate to grow even wider.

I've stood by as it played out. I've seen a woman nearly wreck her life with drugs and alcohol and parties, and when confronted, she simply replied, "I'm struggling to make it like

---

[52] This was allegedly said by Plato, but more likely Ian Maclaren, a Scottish writer and theologian of the 19th century.

everyone else." I've seen cheating husbands who say, "I'm struggling with lust." I've seen pastors who are jerks to their staff and their wives and their children say, "Ministry is such a struggle." I've seen fellow Christians give themselves so many loopholes by trying to play up this gray area — and this actually downsizes God to some kind of doting, bemused grandfather who approves of your first world indulgence.

And let's consider the opposite case. When it's most appropriate to use these terms, we instead beat up the broken people. In church culture, we wrongly believe that suffering from depression is "immoral." We say that anxiety is "not trusting God." We say that "it's wrong to doubt God and ask questions." We say that sickness is "not enough faith." In the church world, your problem is *your* fault and my problem is "struggling."

My dear friend: You already know if you've been hijacking this language for your own justification. It's childish, stubborn deception. I don't mean to be so cruel: but that's the problem, isn't it? **We're afraid to confront the depth of our own ugliness.** We're afraid to own up and take responsibility for it. It's romantic to want a "limp" with a lifelong affliction, because it gets you cool-points to be the guy with a story.

Struggling denotes that there is an uphill climb toward a destination of freedom. It is absolutely destructive to use that word for anything else. We are mocking others with this word if we abuse it one too many times.

I beg of us to not deceive ourselves.

I refuse to say "struggle" when it's so clearly just my flesh.

I refuse to say "defeated" when it was my own poor choice.

I will not say "brokenness" to mean "helplessness."

When Everyone's An Expert On Your Pain

When it comes to mental illness, this line between struggling and selfishness gets murky and gray.

I've suffered from depression my whole life. I don't mean to speak for all mental illness. I can only tell you that my propensity to be depressed did not feel like a choice.

When a celebrity takes his or her own life, everyone on social media suddenly becomes a Google Expert. Most conservative circles would say that depression is a moral matter, while liberal circles would say we're permanently wired with our dispositions.

But is it really this simple?

One side says it's a disease; the other side, a choice.

"He chose to take his own life."

"He couldn't help it."

Many assume it's more of a choice instead of a disease, but it's difficult to explain how even our choices under depression feel hopeless and powerless. Unless you've been at the verge of this inescapable prison, it will naturally seem over-dramatic and hysterical. No one understands it unless it's them, at the absolute edge of their darkness feeling like there are zero options left.

In my early twenties, there was a long stretch of life where I would wake up at three in the afternoon, watch television in random spurts of odd channels, eat a cold dinner, and stay up on the internet until the sun came up. This went on for a long time. I can't recall *years* of my life back then. When I think back, it's just a slate of lit-up screens and tupperware leftovers. I couldn't taste anything. There are no colors in those memories.

I did try to get out of it. I got a girlfriend. I got a job. I moved to another city. I started college again. I partied. None of it worked. If by "worked" I mean finding happiness. I was a ghost in motion, gripping the walls, following signs and getting pushed along by the wind. I pretended to laugh. I did what people asked, I nodded at the right times, I joined conversations and contributed my opinion. Just as quickly as I saw colors, everything turned back to gray.

At some point I was waking up at five in the evening. I was detached even from the possibility of what I was feeling; I saw myself at an arm's distance, never certain of my own existence. People would say words and I would look past their faces, into the space behind. I just wasn't there.

Was this selfishness? Was this just a first world problem? Would I be free of mental illness if I grew up in a third world country?

I'm not sure. But it's a hypothetical non-sequitur. I *didn't* grow up in a different place with different resources. I am here now, forced to confront the inside of my own turmoil.

I can't presume to speak for all sufferers or all conditions. I can only speak for myself when I say, at the very least, *Please hear me. Please take this seriously. Please try to understand. Please do not dismiss me.* Please acknowledge the complexities of the mentally ill person. It goes beyond disease and choice; it goes beyond parts and symptoms, towards the whole.

My only hope is that in our discussions about mental illness, we would remember it involves a real person, who cannot be simplified nor just "snap out of it." If you tell a sufferer of mental illness that it's entirely within their power to get better, then you're inadvertently taking away their power. I cannot control when depression hits. It's not a "feeling" that I can turn off. There isn't enough medicine in the world to cure me. I will live with it for the rest of my life. This isn't sexy or fun or made for TV. It's absolutely debilitating and devastating. I have begged God to kill me. I've prayed for a car accident to take my life. I have sometimes wept all day or slept for fourteen hours. It's not pretty.

The only thing I *can* control despite the overwhelming choke-hold are the stream of little choices each second, to breathe one more time. Though I don't think my illness was a choice, I could still choose to do something about it. It's not a matter of choosing my way out, but choosing against myself, and sometimes even putting that power in other peoples' hands. I'm blessed to know people who don't pretend to understand, but will not refuse me.

We need that safety. We need space for dialogue. Words alone cannot heal, but they can build bridges for the wounded.

> *"And we urge you, brothers,*
> *warn those who are idle,*
> *encourage the timid, help the weak,*
> *be patient with everyone."*
> — 1 Thessalonians 5:14

Perspective:
Breaking Brokenness

I do believe that brokenness is real.

I think addiction can be a near-impossible monster to overcome. Anyone suffering from depression or suicidal thoughts or anxiety shouldn't have to constantly explain themselves. We can be broken by traumatic events or sexual abuse or catastrophic changes.

Which means that the word "broken" has even *more* reason not to be twisted for my agenda.

I believe that brokenness only tells half the story. We are both *broken* and *selfish,* and both can feed into each other. We are not merely products of our environment, but these things are not entirely our fault. It's often a mixture of both.

—

I have a friend who I'll call Tyler.

He suffers from schizophrenia, paranoid delusions, and manic depressive illness.

He has psychotic episodes where he mutters to himself for hours, becomes hostile and violent, and accuses people of time-traveling from the future to steal his ideas.

I've helped him for years and years, landing him jobs and lending him money and giving him a place to stay. I've taken him to the hospital over and over. I've called the cops on him just as many times.

Tyler was fun and cheerful. He was extremely talented and had modeled, consulted for businesses, and did professional web design. I knew that Tyler had a painful childhood. His dad fired a gun at him several times and his mom mostly avoided him. Tyler had been in jail frequently, and he was abused in the worst ways possible. I can't imagine the trauma he's carried beneath his mental illness. I could understand why it was so hard for him to be stable. His breakdowns were very real. He took medicine to shut out the voices in his head.

At the same time, he could be brutally malicious. He liked under-aged girls. He spent hours looking at porn. He was an angry drunk. He was racist. He consistently made poor choices about his work, his money, and his living situation. When he would get a job, he would end up yelling at the boss or fighting with a co-worker, because in his words, "No one can tell me what to do." When he would get money, he would buy shirts and jewelry and new phones from eBay. He would find another place to stay, but end up in altercations with the landlord. These were completely lucid moments when he wasn't having an episode. He hated authority and he was negative about life. I was often his only friend.

I believe Tyler truly, truly struggled. There's no doubt about his condition. But I also believe he had a very small window of choice — and he squandered it all the time. Tyler would be the first to tell you that he sometimes hid behind his illness to escape responsibility. He compared his problems to others as an excuse to be destructive. His pain was very real, but so was his selfishness.

I can't speak for everyone like Tyler. His illness is not his fault. I will never fully comprehend what he's going through, and I don't bring up his story as a cautionary tale.

I only mean to say that our suffering doesn't permit us to be selfish. I'd hope we wouldn't misappropriate certain buzzwords as a cop-out. We would be doing a disservice to those who actually don't have that window of choice.

The bottom line is that I still helped Tyler. He really was suffering, and no amount of his selfishness was going to stop me from leaning into his life.

I don't say that to brag. I wanted to give up many, many times. I made many wrong decisions regarding his care. I never considered myself his "savior." There were times when I cut him off and kept my distance. But even if his suffering had been completely his own fault, I couldn't judge him for this.

Both struggling and selfishness point to legitimate needs. Both the pampered child and the persecuted refugee need the same grace. Their degrees of suffering are different: but if I dismiss one over the other, I am saying one person is less valuable than the other.

My struggle is real. And I am just as selfish.

What will speak to both?

THE PROBLEM WITH JOB:

As we bleed,
we find our
deepest need

[INTERLUDE 3]

Interlude 3
The Problem With Job:
As We Bleed, We Find Our Deepest Need

3:11 — *"Why did I not perish at birth,*
and die as I came from the womb?"

16:7, 9 — *"Surely, O God, you have worn me out;*
you have devastated my entire household ...
God assails me and tears me in his anger
and gnashes his teeth at me ..."

19:6-7 — *"God has wronged me and drawn his net around me.*
Though I cry, 'I've been wronged!'
I get no response; though I call for help, there is no justice."

30:19-21 — *"He throws me into the mud,*
and I am reduced to dust and ashes.
I cry out to you, O God, but you do not answer; I stand up,
but you merely look at me. You turn on me ruthlessly;
with the might of your hand you attack me."

In every book about pain, we eventually have to talk about Job. He's the poster boy for the ever-faithful servant of God who never complained. Except he complained. A lot. And he had every reason to shake his fist.

Job is a man sifted and stripped down to his barest core.

In all his loss, his hurt pointed out the rawest human condition: and perhaps even the vaguest outline of a solution.

Before we get there, the Problem with the Book of Job is that it hardly explains itself. The little that it does explain is horrific: it appears God and Satan have a made a bet over Job's life, as a vehicle to prove that you can take away everything from a man and he would still be a man. This is a neat idea, until you realize the implication that God could be doing this to everyone.

We're left hanging with no rationale.

The Book of Job then is about *preparation,* not explanation. It simply shows that life can be unpredictable, unreasonable, and unfair. Most scholars say that Job was the first written book of the Bible, even before Genesis, so if you believe God orchestrated the Bible down to its order, then God was getting us ready for this. For *exquisite* pain, the kind that has you crawling.

Instead of answering the *why* of our hurt, we're given some resourceful pieces of wisdom to help us endure it. Along the way, we're also given **clues** that tap into an even bigger picture. They're sprinkled throughout, pulsing off the pages of Scripture, like hints to a twist ending. Job began to grasp this in flashes of understanding; he found the imprint of our deepest human need. When he had nothing left, he found something deeper still. The Book of Job prepares us for hard times, but it's preparing us for something else, too. A solution.

This isn't to take away from Job's very real pain. But maybe if Job were here with us, over coffee, on the other end of his pain: he would let us know a few things.

We'll put this trail of bread crumbs together.

The First Clue:
The Problem With Praising God For The Good Stuff

I've always been scared of talking about Job to hurting people because it opens the dark possibility that *bad things can happen to good people and good things can happen to bad people, randomly without order to blatantly lopsided degrees.*

As I write this, one of the news headlines on my Facebook feed reads:

"Registered Sex Offender Wins $3 Million Lottery."

Things like this happen all the time, and it confuses me. Months of work get burned up in a house fire or computer crash. Church roofs collapse. Sinkholes take homes. For as many times as we claim a miracle has happened, we can just as quickly claim that the universe hates us.

Job might have gotten along with Asaph from Psalm 73, who saw that every wicked person was living better off than the righteous.

> **73:3-6, 12-13** — *"For I envied the arrogant when I saw the prosperity of the wicked. They have no struggles; their bodies are healthy and strong. They are free from the burdens common to man; they are not plagued by human ills. Therefore pride is their necklace; they clothe themselves with violence ... This is what the wicked are like— always carefree, they increase in wealth. Surely in vain have I kept my heart pure; in vain have I washed my hands in innocence."*

All of this points to an unsettling truth: that there's no direct correlation between good behavior and good results. This doesn't give a logical answer for the suffering person, and I don't think it's supposed to.

At the end, God shows up and essentially tells Job, "This is not your fault."

God doesn't answer why it happened, but He makes sure to emphasize: *The bad stuff didn't happen because you were bad.*

This is huge. If you're unjustly suffering through devastating pain, I don't want you to think you did something to deserve it. The Book of Job proves that. I don't want you to believe that if you've done bad things, that you're doomed beyond redemption. This also means that we can't connect every good thing that happens to being a "good person."

When someone says, "Life is great and God is good," it sounds like they're saying, "God is good when *my* life is great." When someone thanks God that a hurricane just missed their city, I keep thinking, "What about those people who did get hit? Too bad for them?" When someone thanks God for their blessing, I wonder, "What about those starving kids who are dying by the thousands? Does God just hate them?"

When our thankfulness is attached to things we can gain or lose, then we're determining our value based on our surroundings, and this is a never-ending game of swinging between prideful self-inflation or fist-shaking despair. I don't think that's really gratitude, either.

I'm not saying we stop thanking God for good things. If I win the lottery today, I'm going to thank God all the way to the bank. I thank God for Cuban food. But when we "praise God" only during good times, we inadvertently imply that God is rewarding us for our performance and simultaneously punishing those who are suffering. It's the worst kind of self-fulfilling prophecy. As unfair as life can be, I believe it's even more unfair to tell someone that their good fortune is because God somehow favors them.

It's certainly a problem that the Book of Job doesn't explain his pain. But it would present an even bigger problem if the universe paid us all equally according to our deeds, with a precise ratio, pound for pound for pound. The rich would get richer but the poor would be undone. The Book of Job inversely proves that *no such ratio exists*. Disasters do not equate to God's wrath, as much as blessings do not always equate to God's favor.

I believe Job was free of these kinds of expectations.

We're told that *Job did not charge God with wrongdoing*. Job did not blame himself nor did he blame God for what was happening. Job didn't assume he had lost his "reward" or that he was being "punished." He didn't know why he was suffering such terrible things, but he refused to conclude that God was paying him back.

Since Job did not hate God nor hate himself, he could grieve for what happened instead of making false connections. He did not attach his situation to his self-worth. **It was the purest kind of grief, a freedom to really feel what he was feeling**. Job was angry and he wept and he bled, but it was without shame or bitterness.

I know this might not do anything for you today. If you're hurting right now, I know this is too much talk, and I never want to rush past your healing. But at the very least, even if you're suffering the consequences of something you brought upon yourself — you're not bound to every infraction you've ever made. You're not doomed to karmic retaliation. You don't have to scramble for the good and compensate for your bad. You're free to grieve without self-shaming. When things happen, good or bad, they are things that happen to you, and while they can be tough, they are *not* you.

It's in letting go of our expectancy that we can begin to pursue a life above what happens to us.

The Second Clue:
To Be Truly Human

There's a key line in the first chapter that does not explain our pain, but drops another heavy clue about human nature. It circles back to the earlier problem: *Do we only thank God when life is good?*

Satan asks God, *"Does Job fear God for nothing?"*

In other words, *Is Job only being good because he's got it good?*

God could've replied, "You got me, Satan. That's probably true for every human being down there. They all have an agenda." But God says, "No way. Job is better than that."

Timothy Keller says that Job was shown to be a "free lover of God," that he didn't love God for the benefits but "God for himself alone."[53]

I'm not saying for a moment that God allowed pain to show Job's true colors. I can't speak that far. But we do see Job's true

---

[53] Timothy Keller, *Walking with God through Pain and Suffering* (NY: Penguin, 2013) pp. 273, 275

colors. It seems here that God is describing the purest motive, to *do something for nothing.* Not to be based on conditions or contracts, but *just-because.* Even when we get nothing.

This points to another truth. If I only do good things to get good things back, I'm not sure how good I could really be. If I'm only a good person to get a "divine reward" at the end, I'm not sure I'm a good person. In other words: *If the only reason we're good is to get good back, then it's bad when that's your only reason to be good.*

If I tell the truth because I'm afraid of being dishonest, I'm not really being honest. If I'm nice to someone to get my way, I'm not really being nice to them. Tim Keller says it like this: "What if you fell in love with someone who seemed to love you back, but then when you had a financial reversal, he or she broke off the relationship? Wouldn't you feel used?"[54]

It wouldn't be altruism, but opportunism. It's leveraging everything for my benefit. Such idolatry enslaves us; it objectifies people into stepping stones; we become controlled by ulterior motives; we trick our hearts into doing the right thing, which can't be right at all.

None of us are above this. We all do "something for something." We always have some kind of angle.

Job turned out to have none. He displayed what it means to be truly human. *It's to stay faithful even if you're getting nothing back.* It's to serve anyway. To love anyway. To forgive anyway. To pray anyway. To keep going anyway.

When you are free to do something for nothing, you are also free from everything. Not fully free, and not pain-free, but free to be truly *you* even when you're down to nothing.

---

[54] Ibid., 273

Again, this doesn't solve Job's suffering. It's still a question mark in my mind. What happened to Job was excessive and appalling. Job is angry about what happens to him, as he should be. He endured anyway.

"You may not control all the events that happen to you, but you can decide not to be reduced by them."[55]
— Maya Angelou

The Third Clue: The One Thing That Job's Friends Got Right

The Book of Job is also an intriguing exercise on what *not* to do. A lot of the Old Testament is the same: we're not given prescriptions, but warnings. It's like learning in reverse.

Job's friends show us the worst thing you can do if your friend is hurting.

If you have a friend who's suffering right now, there's one thing I want you to know.

You can either be the voice that someone has to overcome, or you can be the voice that helps to overcome.

Job's friends were convinced that Job had done something wrong to be wronged. It made rational sense to have the ratio. They blamed Job simply for being Job. You've probably heard in sermons how Job's friends were proven wrong by God Himself, who shows up in the final chapter and says, *"I am angry with you*

---

[55] Maya Angelou, *Letter To My Daughter* (NY: Random House, 2008) p. xii

and your two friends, because you have not spoken of me what is right, as my servant Job has."

The most remarkable thing here is that Job spoke *what is right* of God. For all of Job's flailing and frustration and shock, he was right to yell out.

But maybe even more remarkable is that Job's friends got one thing right. It's not what they said, but what they didn't.

> **2:12-13** — *When they saw [Job] from a distance, they could hardly recognize him; they began to weep aloud, and they tore their robes and sprinkled dust on their heads. Then they sat on the ground with him for seven days and seven nights. No one said a word to him, because they saw how great his suffering was.*

There's certainly a time to speak. God did that when He showed up.

But there's also a time to weep. Your friend needs this, and so do you.

That also means I don't need to talk heavy theology all the time. I don't need to talk about my hurt whenever you're here. It doesn't always have to be morbid and dreary and grave. Sometimes I just need Netflix and ice cream and a greasy hamburger with you. Sometimes your friend needs you to force them to get dressed, go to that revival, go to that birthday party, go to the charity, go to the gym. I want to ice skate and fall down. I want the dumb movie. I want chicken noodle soup, and not a cup, but the bowl. Your friend needs sweat pants and pictures of cats. I need you to get ready for one moment of laughter and the next moment of tears. But mostly, we need to see the colors again, even through the weeping.

Often the best theology your friend needs right now is you. Not more lectures or advice. You're the miracle they're praying for.

The Fourth Clue: Intimate and Glorious

God shows up in the last five chapters of Job in a roaring storm.

Before I go on, let's consider that for a second. You're with your friends, at the mall or at school or at work, having a theological discussion about evil and tragedy and atrocity, and then God shows up. In a storm. Thunder and lightning. Howling wind. Beating rain. Indoors.

I think many of us have the idea that we'd put "God on trial" to answer for what He's done. And maybe each of us will get our day in court. We'll get to ask God some things. We can air our grievances. We'll even point a finger.

But every time God shows up in the Bible, people fall over crying. Moses had to hide in a mountain.[56] Ezekiel fell on his head.[57] Isaiah wanted to die.[58] Jacob dislocated his hip.[59] Peter, James, and John went to their faces.[60] The Roman guards were blasted.[61] Paul was slapped off his horse.[62] John nearly fell over dead.[63]

---

[56] Exodus 33:19-23
[57] Ezekiel 1:28
[58] Isaiah 6
[59] Genesis 32
[60] Matthew 17:1-9, Mark 9:2-8, Luke 9:28-36
[61] John 18:6

God tells Moses, "No man may see Me and live."

Why?

Because in the presence of overwhelming greatness, we are reduced to quivering ashes.

The greater someone is, the more I see flaws in myself. You might get jealous at a slightly better singer or writer or dancer or artist — but when that person is levels beyond you, a *prodigy*, you're blown away by their sheer astronomical talent. Even in the presence of human power, we're overwhelmed by insecurity and humility.[64]

Think of every Godzilla movie you've ever watched. Those tiny frantic people in the street can only run. And they run into places that Godzilla can turn into toothpicks.

If someone Infinitely Glorious were to rip the roof off your home and peer in: you'd have to collect your jaw and change your shorts. You'd probably burst into flames. You'd be as naked as the day you were born.

The amazing thing here is that when *God shows up,* Job does not catch on fire. He's not torn to pieces by the wind. He doesn't wet himself. God shows up in all His glory, but it was His very glory that held Job from imploding into shreds.

Even more, God *answers* Job out of the storm. The normal Hebrew word should've been "spoken to," which means a one-way monologue. But the Hebrew word used here is to *reply*. God invites Job into a two-way discussion, a dialogue. And the last

---

[62] Acts 9:1-9

[63] Revelation 1:17

[64] Inspired by a sermon from Timothy Keller, "The Gospel." Preached at Redeemer Presbyterian Church. September 25th, 2005

spoken words in the Book of Job are from Job himself — he gets the last word.

This reminds me of 1 Kings 19, when Elijah the prophet, who is suicidal and near his breaking point, meets God at a mountain. We're told,

> "... *A great and powerful wind tore the mountains apart and shattered the rocks before the LORD, but the LORD was not in the wind. After the wind there was an earthquake, but the LORD was not in the earthquake. After the earthquake came a fire, but the LORD was not in the fire. And after the fire came **a gentle whisper.**"*

God is shown as both **Infinitely Glorious** and **Graciously Intimate** at the same time.

He is unbearably holy, but He is *for* you.

God tells Job, "Brace yourself" — and He flexes His power for five chapters. Yet God has shown up to restore Job, too. We're still not told why Job had to hurt so badly: but we see that the God who could reduce us to ashes is by our side, eye-to-eye, and invites us into this glory. It's such glory that overwhelms even Job's pain, because in the presence of a greatness that is *for* us, we are wrapped in a beauty that can engulf our deepest wounds. Such beauty doesn't erase the pain, but can expel it by sheer force. The right musical note, the perfect meal, a cloudless sky, a masterful work of art: none of these things are compensation for our hurt, but they're just big enough to turn down the volume on everything else. A powerful love can make the dark a little less encompassing.

The Bigger Picture:
Something For Nothing

In the end, I think the Book of Job is a graphic depiction of the reality of life. I will never get to the bottom of it, and each time I've read it, it has left me sleepless.

But when we put all the clues together, we find a man in the worst kind of pain reaching for the most fundamental of needs. A person in despair only demands the essentials. In a sense, Job was forced to prioritize what was most important. He began to sculpt them into a shape.

The first need, or clue, was that he wanted fairness in life. The second was to be truly himself, to do "something for nothing." The third was for a True Friend. The fourth was for a love that was both powerful and personal.

Throughout the book, Job makes several enigmatic statements crying out for all these things — and they make up another clue. He points to a real person.

> **9:33-34** — *If only there were someone to arbitrate between us, to lay his hand upon us both, someone to remove God's rod from me, so that his terror would frighten me no more.*

> **16:19-21** — *Even now my witness is in heaven; my advocate is on high. My intercessor is my friend as my eyes pour out tears to God; on behalf of a man he pleads with God as a man pleads for his friend.*

In Job's lifetime, he did get a glimpse of all this together. In the final chapter, Job was vindicated. All the accusations against him by his friends were reversed. God showed up, both powerful and personal. Job was repaid in full with a new family, new livestock, a renewed life. His world was set right again.

But the bigger problem with Job is that his suffering was not the final problem. He was innocent, but he was not perfect. Even when his pain was over, he was still stuck; he would need a mediator who could clear him of *all* condemnation.

In the first clue, we found that good things often happen to "bad" people and bad things happen to "good" people. This is an unfair reality that we want re-ordered. Yet — if God actually repaid every single person for all they did, who could really stand under such examination?

The Book of Job is not really about that. But as each external layer of Job is stripped away, he cries out for more than just rescue. He doesn't ask for only a ceasing of his pain, but for *redemption*. He wants total justice for all that has gone wrong — but he knows that such a justice would undo him. He couldn't have his cake and eat it, too.

We are strugglers, but we are also selfish.

We want fairness in the world, but if even just one person got what was really fair — "God, pay back that guy! God, give me what I deserve!" — the ripple effect throughout humanity would completely annihilate us.

Job needed a mediator who wouldn't count him against him. Someone who could really do something for nothing. A true friend. Glorious, yet close enough to the pain to carry us.

Is it possible that we're all looking for the same thing?

Is it possible we're looking for a mediator to reverse the accusations?

Is it possible that this same mediator would be the friend by our side? Our friend through pain? The way to a renewed life?

And perhaps such a Mediator already exists.

One who stood in the way of condemnation,

one who was falsely accused, not just by friends, but by enemies who cursed him to die,

one who cried out *Why* and received no response,

one who was not only by our side, but suffered alongside,

one who was both glorious and intimate,

one who truly did something for nothing —

and brought about a renewal of all that had ever gone wrong, to set our world right again, while keeping us whole and intact.

I'm trying to imagine if such a man truly were to truly do this for us, without conditions or contracts or agendas, and how it would so enlarge my heart to face this unfair world.

If someone could bear it together: it might be this much more bearable.

"Are you dying for him?" she whispered.

"And his wife and child. Hush! Yes."

"O you will let me hold your brave hand, stranger?"

"... Keep your eyes upon me, dear child, and mind no other object."

"I mind nothing while I hold your hand. I shall mind nothing when I let it go."

— *A Tale of Two Cities*, when Sydney takes Darnay's place on death row, and he meets a sentenced woman alongside him.

IMAGINE YOU MADE THE WORLD:

How would you save it?

[CHAPTER 6]

Chapter 6
Imagine You Made The World:
How Would You Save It?

"The Bible paints a picture of a certain evil tricking innocent humans into betraying the God who loved them, the King who was their friend. They were enticed, they considered their options, and they wanted to be equal to God. It's ugly stuff.

"... You and I were not supposed to be this way. As creatures in need of somebody outside ourselves to name us, as creatures incomplete outside the companionship of God, our souls are born distorted, I am convinced of it. I am convinced that Moses was right, that his explanation was greater than Freud's or Maslow's or Pavlov's. I believe, without question, that none of us are happy in the way we were supposed to be happy. I believe that nobody on this planet is so secure, so confident in their state that they feel the way Adam and Eve felt in the Garden, before they knew they were naked. I believe we are in the wreckage of a war, a kind of Hiroshima, a kind of Mount Saint Helens, with souls distorted like the children of Chernobyl. As terrible as it is to think about these things, as ugly as it is to face them, I have to see the world this way in order for it to make sense. I have to believe something [terrible] happened, and we are walking around holding our wounds."[65]

— Donald Miller

[65] Donald Miller, *Searching For God Knows What* (TN: Thomas Nelson, 2004, 2010) pp. 82, 87-88

The Word Which Shall Not Be Spoken

There's a problem before our problem.

If we truly want God to set this world right, to conquer evil and heal pain and smite injustice, then we immediately run into a Cosmic Dilemma.

I want God to destroy the evil in this world: but could He destroy evil without destroying me? If God healed all that was wrong with the world, would I be wiped away, too?

We could say it like this. "Without a God of justice, what hope is there for the world? But with a God of justice, what hope is there for you and for me?"[66]

This involves a word I haven't used yet through this entire journey, because it's such a loaded, divisive word.

That word is **sin.**

Many of us see this as an outdated, archaic term, and it's often used as a punch-line at parties. You won't see it in textbooks or headlines. No one says that Hitler sinned or that the Nazis were sinners. The word is even considered offensive and unproductive.

On the other hand, the church culture throws around this term with too much aplomb. When we think of sin, we think of the obvious dramatic stuff: lying to your boss, domestic abuse, spousal adultery, cooking meth. But if the external stuff was the problem, then most of us would be okay. Most church people do not own a meth lab.

The idea of sin is often seen as disobedience, but I think it runs much deeper than that.

---

[66] Timothy Keller, interview with Collin Hansen on The Gospel Coalition

When we read about Original Sin, we read that Adam and Eve were tricked and they turned away from God and realized they were naked. I notice a lot of preachers here say, "They sinned, they disobeyed!" — which is true. But the reason why Adam and Eve and everyone else sins is not because we're doing bad things. Sin causes us to do bad things, sure, but it's not about the external action.

Sin is not merely disobedience, but a *disconnection*. It is our nakedness and vulnerability.

Sin is not just disobedience against God and how we're made, but also a disconnection from the all-fulfilling love and glory of God. Such disconnection, the Bible implies, is the root cause of our suffering in the world.

The story of Adam and Eve tells us we once had all the love and glory we could ever want — but because of sin, we are now disconnected from the source. We are floating in the "forever empty." We are exiles in search of a memory: the image of the glorious.

The word glory in Hebrew is **chabod,** which means "weight" and implies a kind of qualitative value. When we "glorify" something, it means, "This has substantial worth and it's critical to my existence."

We're told that God is the truest, purest glory in the universe.[67] *We were made to be filled by His glory and His alone.* In sermons when I talk about glory, I sometimes say as a joke, "God is not just the only weight, but He's overweight. He's more than all we need." When humanity turned away from God, as the

---

[67] Isaiah 40 and mostly the rest of the Bible.

Genesis story goes, we also *disconnected* from the weight of our very existence.

We once had the voice of God constantly telling us we were loved, approved, affirmed, and validated. But we chose apart from God, and ever since *we've been looking for glory in everything else that isn't God.*

Ever since Adam and Eve messed up, we've been looking for God in things that are not Him. We've been trying to find wholeness in things that can't fill us. It's not so much that our sinful behavior is bad, but it's a symptom of a much larger problem. We were designed for God's infinite glory, but we're now trying to find glory in lesser stuff.

Our legitimate need for glory turns into illegitimate methods of glory-hogging. It can mean addiction or codependency or selling out for fame. It could mean too much sex and too much money. Our internal disconnection manifests into external disobedience.

C.S. Lewis says:

> *"What Satan put into the heads of our remote ancestors was the idea that they could 'be like god'—could set up on their own as if they had created themselves—be their own masters—invent some sort of happiness for themselves outside God, apart from God. And out of that hopeless attempt has come nearly all that we call human history—money, poverty, ambition, war, prostitution, classes, empires, slavery—the long terrible story of man trying to find something other than God which will make him happy."*

Nearly every human problem can be traced back to the desperate search for our own glory. But all human glory is temporary, hence the human problem.

We try to squeeze from people and from things what only God can give us. We build a kingdom of self because we're apart from the True King. We either use each other as "vehicles" or attack each other as "obstacles." These expectations crush others and crush ourselves, and in a way, it breaks the heart of God.[68]

Sin is not just between people, but also so pervasive that it causes *personal iniquities* when we're alone, like vanity and self-hate and anxiety, and *planetary dysfunction,* which is why our earth doesn't work like it's supposed to. In every way, from soul to stars to molecules, our whole existence is shriveled by this disease called sin. We are a creation who runs and hides from our Creator to go our own way.

If you're in pain right now, I can tell you just enough advice to get you to the other side. But if we're to arrive at a *Final Answer,* an ending that re-rights every wrong in history, we come to a gridlock. It's a stand-off.

Before we talk about the evil and suffering and pain in this world, we at least must admit this up front: *part of the problem in this world is you and me.* We have contributed to our fallen nature. If God were to erase all pain, He would eventually find His way back to us.

I know that if you come from a Western culture, this really bothers you. A Westerner would say that all suffering is unjust and that "God owes me." But Easterners (like me) have no problem with this. The Eastern culture would say that all suffering *is* just, because fate or karma is paying you back. A part of you knows this is partially right, because if you or your family have ever been affected by a violent crime, you expect the law to win.

---

[68] The "kingdom of self" is inspired by Paul David Tripp.

It's only the narrative of the Bible that says suffering is both unjust *and* just, because on one hand, our pain is absolutely not a part of the design, but on the other hand, we expect God to utterly defeat all that is vile and oppressive.

This idea of a Disconnected Universe also puts our responsibility in the right place, by not shaming us for our struggles but clearly calling out our selfishness. On one hand, we are not entirely at fault for our condition, because we entered the world long after it was fallen and eroded. Much of our suffering is simply standing in a stream of broken glass that came before us. When you see disease and disaster and even death, you see by-products of a misshapen world. If this is true, then God suffers when you suffer. I don't believe that God is waiting for you to "get it" or to spiritualize your tragedy into an afterschool special. So often, our hurt is pure unprovoked pain. It is not sinful, but comes from sin.

On the other hand, suffering was a consequence of a terrible human choice. It was never meant to be this way. The first people kicked over the dominos of creation, affecting a chain reaction of disarrayed satellites pointing in the wrong direction. If you and I had been the first humans: it wouldn't have been long until we did the same thing. And though we have the free will to improve our condition, which we often do, we also continue to provoke more pain by exploitation, power-plays, and stealing glory from one another.

Sin broke us, yet we keep choosing sin.

This must be why Jesus prayed, "Let your will be done on earth as it is in Heaven."

Why would he teach us to pray this? Unless: *God doesn't always get what He wants.*

I can't imagine having His job, trying to intervene so we could have our very best without infringing on our free will. I'm almost certain He has intervened for us an innumerable amount of times beyond our knowledge, but if He intervened every single time, we would never get a thought off the ground.

God would need a way to bring justice without utterly destroying what He has made.

He would need to be a love so powerful that it would cure our pain, but a justice so wide that it would lay waste to evil. Sin and suffering are so intertwined that love could not be love without justice. For God to truly love us, He would need to be angry at what hurts us: and so often, what hurts us is *us*.

As a pilot once told me, "It's a sh_tty world out there. Full of pain, full of thugs. Who would even save it?"

We need healing *and* we need forgiveness.

And you cannot have a God of healing without a God of justice.

There is our predicament.

"Ecclesiastes 3:11 says that God 'has put eternity into man's heart.' At some level, in the deepest part of our soul, our soul remembers … what life was like before the fall. At some really deep level, our soul has this impression cut into it by the fingers of God, like the grooves on a record, encoding the memory of what it was like before sin entered the world. We remember, at a really deep level, that at one time we were full, and at one time we were happy, and at one time there was nothing weighing us down. Our souls are outright groaning to get back there."[69]
— Matt Chandler

---

[69] Matt Chandler, *The Explicit Gospel* (IL: Crossway, 2012) p. 129

Jesus: Miracle Healer By Day, Crime-Fighter By Night

Jesus, the man who claimed to be the Son of God, did a really weird thing during his three and a half year ministry. He went around healing all kinds of people: lepers, the lame, the blind, the deaf, the mute, the demon-possessed and the terminally ill. But almost every time he performed a miracle, he would say, "I forgive you" or "I'm from God."

In Mark 2, when the paralyzed man is lowered through the roof of the house, the first thing Jesus says to him is, "Your sins are forgiven." And then he heals him.

In John 6, Jesus feeds five-thousand hungry people by multiplying bread and fish, but then he tells the following crowds, "I am the bread of life. Whoever comes to me will never go hungry, and whoever believes in me will never be thirsty."

In John 11, Jesus goes to revive his dead friend Lazarus. He consoles Lazarus's sister Mary by weeping with her, but then tells the other sister Martha, "I am the resurrection and the life. The one who believes in me will live, even though they die; and whoever lives by believing in me will never die."

In Mark 5, maybe one of my absolute favorite stories in the gospels, Jesus casts out a multitude of demons named Legion who had possessed a man living in the Decapolis, the Ten Cities. Jesus expels these demons into about two-thousand pigs on the hillside, and the pigs all run off the cliff into the water, drowning themselves.

You have to imagine this scene for a moment. The disciples are waiting on a boat near the hill, watching Jesus enter this haunted town where a demon-possessed man had been living in a cemetery, stalking the people, howling every night, cutting himself with rocks. The disciples see Jesus climb to the hillside, a tiny figure on the promontory, who is suddenly jumped by the demoniac. But the man falls to his knees. Jesus yells, *"Exelthe tu pneuma tu akatharton!"* This isn't to cast out Legion yet, but to force him to reveal himself.

I'm wondering what this looked like. Imagine a plume of swirling black smoke exploding out of the demon-possessed man, rising into the clouds, thousands of demons twisting in the air. Jesus says, "What is your name?" The demons answer, in a hideous cacophony of voices, "We are Legion, for we are many."

Then the mass of demons is driven into the pigs, and there go two-thousand pink barrels floating in the water, their nostrils shooting bubbles and blood.

When the townspeople catch up, they should be overjoyed. The demoniac has been healed, the town is now free — but the town has been carrying a dark secret.

If you didn't know, the Jewish people in this day didn't eat pork. No bacon, no barbeque. So these two-thousand pigs might have been an illegal pig farming business. It's even possible that the city used the demon-possessed man to cover up the conspiracy.

Jesus came to heal the demoniac, but he also pulverized the sin of the city.

He not only performed an exorcism, but he busted up an illegal pig crack-house.

Why would Jesus do this?

Because though Jesus knew our suffering was very great, our sin was greater still. He could alleviate pain for a day, for a month, for a whole life — but he was even more concerned for our eternity. I know that sounds like the Christian thing to say. *But it's in gaining security for eternity that we can face our suffering today.*

To have such eternal confidence, we need a place where both suffering and sin can be vanquished in one stroke, with laser pin-point accuracy; we need a place to conquer the problem and not the person, to remove the guilt without crushing the guilty.

This is where we land on the Cross.

But I'm A Good Person Though: I Don't Need A Cross

This sin-problem is a big deal, but maybe you don't believe me.

Before we keep looking at the idea of "sin," I think it's more helpful to talk about our idea of "good." In my entire pastoral ministry, I never had difficulty talking about "sin" to the addicts, the ex-convicts, the criminals. They already knew they had messed it up. They knew they needed both healing and atonement.

My difficulty was always with very "good people." What could I say? They weren't in desperate need for correction, for a Savior. They would hear the sermon and say, "Oh yeah, I already do all that stuff." Most people in general are not doing black tar heroin or punching animals.

When I was an atheist, I absolutely believed that everyone was capable of moral good. I still do believe that. My morality back then was simple: I believed we all have a common human decency and we ought to respect each other out of dignity. Anyone who didn't do this was a jerk. I didn't want to be a jerk. I thought this was common sense. If you needed a "God" to love people, then I thought, "You're already a terrible person." I'm not saying every non-religious person believes this: but it's common. Morality is often driven by self.

When I heard about Jesus "dying for my sin," I felt two things.

1) This is absolutely stupid, because I didn't ask for anyone to die for me, and

2) I was aware of the wrong things I did, and so at the very least, Jesus made a pretty nice gesture.

Here's where my logic turned into Swiss cheese,

The Bible made it clear that my self-comparison was merely **self-righteousness**. To say, "I don't want to be a jerk" is still a jerk-ish thing to say, because I'm instantly condemning others. My morality for "common human decency" was rigging my heart by pride, so that my motivation was to look like a good neighbor and upstanding citizen. I would look down on others if they were not.

This goes back to our internal conundrum: *If we're motivated to do good to look good and get good back, then of course, none of this is very good.* We don't do something for nothing.

Some of us are simply "bad" because we fall into being very "good." Trying to escape your life by thrills is just as toxic as trying to elevate yourself by self-will.

We need a **pure motivation**, a piercing kind of goodness that doesn't need self-inflation.

In Colossians 2, Paul doesn't call out the obvious bad things that we do. He says that our drive to be good people is a "deceptive philosophy." It's an inner-flagellation with an "appearance of wisdom" and "self-worship" and "false humility," and it "lacks any value to restrain sensual indulgence." In other words: it's a morality-suit.

The problem isn't so much that I'm a "bad person," but that I need healing from my selfishness. We can do good, but it's always for the wrong reasons. I'm constantly seeking of approval and affirmation by my actions; I long for a love to tell me "You're okay, you did great." We yearn to hear, "Well done." *We want to be both fully known and fully loved.* We're in this desperate sin-filled race of validation.

Now it's true that many of us don't do too many wrong things. But our capacity for evil also runs way deeper than we think. **No one is so bad that they're beyond redemption, but no one is so good that they're beyond corruption.** This is the plotline of nearly every successful movie and TV show, from *Breaking Bad* to *The Dark Knight* to *Rugrats*.

I look at the genocide in Iraq, or the pyramid schemes of CEOs, or the 27 million slaves in the world, and I think, *I'm definitely not as bad as the perpetrators of these crimes. I could never do what they did.*

Then I think of myself in the same situation. I think, *What if I had grown up with the same temptations, upbringing, cultural "values," and corrupted ideologies as the oppressors? Would I be any better than them? Would I really be so much more sophisticated than the worst people in the world?*

You've heard of the Stanley Milgram Experiment.[70] It's quite famous for answering the question, *How could these Nazi "doctors" exterminate so many people but go home to kiss their family?* In other words, *Did the Nazis simply follow orders?* In the experiment, most subjects were willing to electrocute someone against their screams, so long as they were told by an authority figure to keep pressing the button. Sixty-five percent of them kept going even when the subjects "died." I wonder if I would've been in that sixty-five percent.

Do you remember the old *Twilight Zone* episode called "The Monsters Are Due On Maple Street"? This small town has its power shut off at random, and the townspeople blame each other and start looting and setting fires and eventually kill someone. The surprise ending (spoilers) is that aliens were controlling the electricity to see how humans would react if you just shut off a few lights.

At the end, the aliens say this:

> **First Alien:** *Understand the procedure now? Just stop a few of their machines and radios and telephones and lawn mowers, throw them into darkness for a few hours, and then sit back and watch the pattern.*
> **Second Alien:** *And this pattern is always the same?*
> **First Alien:** *With few variations. They pick the most dangerous enemy they can find, and it's themselves. All we need do is sit back and watch.*

And the narrator says this:

> *"The tools of conquest do not necessarily come with bombs and explosions and fallout. There are weapons that are simply thoughts, attitudes, prejudices, to be found only in the minds of men."*

---

[70] Stanley Milgram, "The Journal of Abnormal and Social Psychology," Vol 67(4), Oct 1963, 371-378. http://psycnet.apa.org/journals/abn/67/4/371/

I know it's just a TV show. But read the news long enough and you'll find people just like you and me, who never did a very wrong thing their whole lives, get thrown into a crazy situation and suddenly become the monsters on Maple Street.

All that goes to say: **Each of us is capable of the worst atrocities imaginable, given the proper conflicts and resources and time.** It only takes the quiet bubble of a suburban Westernized neighborhood to truly fool ourselves into thinking we're "good people." When we take away our roofs, our toys, and our laws: we all become the enemy.

In a post-apocalyptic world of zombies like *The Walking Dead,* we're all the Governor. None of us are Rick. None of us are even as good as Carl.

We're all two steps away from utter chaos.

The world is pretty crazy, but maybe we should be astonished that it's not as terrible as it could be. I know who I really am inside. I'm a wretched, wicked, twisted up rebel. I've only been good out of self-righteous motives, which means I've never done any good on my own. None of us are truly altruistic at the core.

We are looking for a *righteousness* outside us, beyond us, supernatural, not from this world, but breaking in, in order to bring healing to a busted up people.

What will heal us?

But more importantly: who will save us?

A Love That Breaks Death, Darkness, and Every Other Love

Imagine with me that you are God. You made people to love you, know your love, and to love each other.

But they turn against you and turn against each other. And all that they once had in you: they look for it from other people, either using them or killing them or both.

Donald Miller imagines the moment that God walks on to the scene after Adam and Eve had turned from Him.

> *"All this makes me wonder what God must have felt, arriving on the scene just after the Fall [of man in Genesis 3], knowing all He had made was ruined, and understanding at once the sacrifice that would be required to win the hearts of His children from the grasp of their seducer. I see Him in my mind walking the paths, calling to the couple, meeting their eyes for the first time, and Adam and Eve shaking in absolute terror, wondering what had happened, confused at the broken promise of a snake, feeling at once the trustworthiness of their first love and wondering if God would ever love them again, feeling the hot breath of His anger and emotion, hearing Him speak for the first time, not as a friend, but as One who had been betrayed. 'Who told you that you were naked?'"*[71]

So what would you do?

I understand if you would punish the world. I understand that those who had wronged each other would owe each other for what they did. Those who had wronged you would owe you endlessly. I understand that you couldn't let anyone get away with anything, or you wouldn't be a good God. I understand discipline, justice, and wrath.

---

[71] Donald Miller, *Searching For God Knows What* (TN: Thomas Nelson, 2004, 2010) p. 86

You have watched the centuries of war, genocide, terrorism, and slavery: some of this in your name. You have seen the greed, lust, jealousy, and anger in their hearts, the plotting of heinous deeds from thoughts to movements to wretched action. You have seen apathy and a blind eye in the plentiful.

Certainly you wouldn't enter the world as one of your own creations, stripped of your own divine power, and walk among these thieves and murderers. You wouldn't take on their weaknesses and infirmities and temptations. Of course you wouldn't dare to teach them the true nature of their original design: that they're to love you, to love each other, that there is another world beyond this one. And you wouldn't give up *your own glory* so that everyone could regain the glory that they already gave up themselves.

But this is what Jesus did.

It's the Biggest Plot Twist of all time.

God is too holy to let sin go unpaid, but He loves us too much to let us pay for it.

The amazing thing to me is that even though we turned away from God's glory, *He still wants us to be part of His story*. In Philippians 2, we're told that the Son of God gave up his God-status and took on human form to become a servant, and in the end even humbled himself to die on a cross. For us. And he was raised again in power, for us. So then every knee will bow, every tongue will confess: *that Jesus Christ is Lord, to the glory of God the Father.*

This last part is important, for both our sin and for suffering. We're called to **re-locate our human glory to its divine source.**

This is crucial for the suffering person, because suffering involves the unpredictable whirlwind of life. It's to be without a home, without an anchor. It's to find that *life itself* does not have the constant glory that we long for. The reason why I would throw my entire weight upon Jesus is because he is not only unshakeable, but he died for me that I might have a home in him.

When I locate the glory back to God, I'm no longer locating my hope in money, marriage, or myself. My hope is not in things "working out" for me. When God is my glory, I can become less shakeable, more pure, more true, more myself. I can actually enjoy things like money and marriage instead of using them to fill my own emptiness. I can finally do something for nothing, with fully free motives. I no longer live under the tyranny of self-dictatorship, in which I hog the glory and steal the limelight. It's because I'm re-connected to the source.

St. Augustine said, *"Our hearts are restless until they find their rest in thee."* A commentator paraphrased this to say, *"Only love of the immutable can bring tranquility."*[72]

In other words: **Only a love you could never lose will bring ultimate peace.** Only a glory that is richer than our fleeting lives could anchor us through trials, through suffering, through the grief and fear of death and the "forever empty," through the worst of the world and ourselves. Only the beauty of sacrificial redemption could ever make us whole in both our sin and our pain.

Tim Keller says, *"The only love that won't disappoint you is one that can't change, that can't be lost, that is not based on the ups and downs of life or of how well you live. It is something that not even death can take away from you. God's love is the only thing like that."*[73]

---

[72] http://www.redeemer.com/redeemer-report/article/why_i_love_gods_immutability
[73] Timothy Keller, *Walking with God through Pain and Suffering* (NY: Penguin, 2013) p. 304

Jesus doesn't answer why bad things happen — but he gives us a love stronger than all that does. He not only offers a glory bigger than anything the earth can offer, but a glory that will outshine all that we have gone through, as but a candle held up to the splendor of the sun.

He Was There: He Is Here

"The early Christians did not say in dismay: 'look what the world has come to,' but in delight, 'look what has come to the world!'"[74]
— E. Stanley Jones

Here's why I believe in the Christian faith.

I believe at some point in human history, God became one of us.

I believe He came as *Yeshua,* a man who was fully God, to reverse the human condition. In just one place, at one time, in the dirtiest sand-swept stain of a city, He healed our entropy as an invitation to His story.

Jesus punched through the impenetrable membrane between a perfectly loving Father and a disastrous deadly people, and so we have a God who has touched the dirt of the earth and met us in our aching slumber.

I believe in Jesus because his life means *God actually showed solidarity with us in our pain.* He didn't come to earth with a flowchart or diagram. He is not less than theology, but he is also our unyielding companion. He is, in fact, more present in our

---

[74] E. Stanley Jones, *Abundant Living* (TN: Abingdon, 1942) p. 183

pain than anywhere else. He has not checked out, but completely checked in. He is the friend who will stay with me side-by-side and hear my venting, embrace my shaking, and love me through my flailing mess. I need a *presence* who can relate to my pain.

At the same time, I need an authority who is strong enough to lead me through the very same hurt. One who is Graciously Intimate, yet Infinitely Glorious. One who understands me, but is somehow above me. I believe in Jesus because he was just like us, but He is in the lead. And yet, he is chair to chair, eye to eye, hand in hand.

The cross also broke our sin without breaking us. **The cross proves that we can be fully known and yet still fully loved.**

At the cross, Jesus absorbed the cycle of human violence. He took on the curse of the hostility of a broken world, for all we could do and have done. He took on the accusations of the devil and evil men. He identified with us by taking on all the harm of sin, though he never sinned himself. Jesus reversed death in a grave so that even death would work backwards through our hearts, and all that sin ruins would be restored and made right. He offers us a union with him by being united with the Spirit of God, so that we can walk with him. He tore down the destructive kingdom of self to once again become our gracious True King. He inaugurated a new kind of Kingdom where the weak can win, the poor can succeed, and all our survival values are flipped into sacrifice.

Jesus redefined what it means to be human by creating an upside-down kingdom where the humble are celebrated and the prideful are melted by love. His love presses into both the *struggling* and the *selfish*. He can break the stubborn sinner as much as He renews the hurting in despair.

Though Jesus had to die for the depth of our sin, he was glad to die for the death of our sin: because he loves us.

This is grace. It is love freely given, *just-because,* but a love that cost everything: the life of God's Son. Without such a cost, it's just sentimental feeling, but with such a cost, it's electrifying power. It at once heals us and pierces us. Grace restores our broken places while also confronting our sin head-on. It meets us in our pain but also revokes our pride. It's the great equalizer which recognizes our desperate human need. It's the unchanging love that changes us; it disturbs our ego and complacency; it is the limitless love that provokes us into the same love. When grace has taken hold, we are finally motivated by the pure motive of no-motive, because our hearts have been punctured by a *just-because* love that expects nothing back.

It's this love that will shake us and re-shape us again.

It's this love that keeps me going —

— *for when I was going through hell, he went through hell with me, and when I reached for Heaven, Heaven had come to me.*

"Through the prism of my tears I have seen a suffering God. It is said of God that no one can behold his face and live. I always thought this meant that no one could see his splendor and live. A friend said perhaps it means that no one could see his sorrow and live. Or perhaps his sorrow is his splendor."[75]
— Nicholas Wolterstorff

---

[75] Nicholas Wolterstorff, *Lament for a Son* (MI: Berdmans, 1987, 2001) p. 81

"The beauty is that he died on the cross for our sins, but also that he existed the way we exist. He understands what it's like to lose a friend. He's not unfamiliar with those emotions. He's not unfamiliar with the difficulty of human life. To me that's what makes Jesus as God beautiful. He totally understands. He went out of his way to prove to us that he understands our situation. So when he has something to say, it's not coming from this high and lofty standpoint. It's coming from this person who understands intricately the perils of human existence."[76]

— John Mark McMillan

For we do not have a high priest who is unable to sympathize with our weaknesses, but we have one who has been tempted in every way, just as we are — yet was without sin.

Let us then approach the throne of grace with confidence, so that we may receive mercy and find grace to help us in our time of need.

— Hebrews 4:15-16

The Redemption of God for the Mission of God: His Glory Brings Us To His Story

"When Jesus was brought to the place where his friend Lazarus lay dead ... he did not offer any solution. He only wept. Then the other things he said and did. But first he simply let his tears be his word."[77]

— Frederick Buechner

You're invited.

You're invited to enter the pain.

When Jesus saw death, he wept. He snorted. He was angry.

---

[76] http://magazine.biola.edu/article/10-fall/worship-creativity-and-a-sloppy-wet-kiss/

[77] Frederick Buechner, *Telling The Truth: The Gospel as Tragedy, Comedy, and Fairy Tale* (NY: HarperCollins, 1977) p. 35

If you're mad at all the suffering in the world: *God is just as mad.* It's good to be angry about this. God is angry at injustice, too. We live in a world that is still fractured, fallen, hostile, and weary. *Nothing in this world is as it ought to be.* "Nothing is yet in its true form," said our brother, C.S. Lewis.

The Christian has every reason to be pessimistic, because sin really exists. Yet the Christian has every reason to be optimistic, because hope really exists. The Christian is both happier and sadder at the same time, the most hurt and the most joyful.[78] We feel the full burden of grief but our joy has no limit. We do not deny the worst of our emotions: but our emotions have a direction.

When you look at the chaos in the world:

We can do something about it.

Jesus invites us to re-do the paint, to pull the thread of sin that is woven in every human heart. We're invited to enter into the fray of others with sleeves rolled up and armed with the strength and mercy of God. Not to have one more theological debate about evil, though we can, and not to write one more blog post defending God, though we're able.

You're invited into the desert to irrigate the dry, cracked places.

Theology is good, but we too quickly say "God has a plan" while people are suffering. It's not incorrect, but it's incomplete. God *does* have a plan, and that was the sending of His Son to redeem this fallen world. It was the inauguration of a Kingdom in which *we are the participants,* and until Jesus comes again, we're called to fight evil in its every form.

---

[78] Inspired by Timothy Keller, from his sermon "The Search for Happiness." Preached at Redeemer Presbyterian Church. September 12th, 1993

Jesus's very presence as God in the flesh means we need less talk, more rescue.

I know we can't save everyone, nor can we fully "move the needle" on poverty and slavery and oppression. **But each of us, by God's grace, has a limited amount of resources and ability and knowledge, to do what we can, where we are, with reckless abandon.**

At times it makes me crazy to see the pain in the world. The more news I read, the more it kills me inside, and I get frustrated that so few of us care. I wonder how we could really think about anything else. The hard part is not to get bitter. Not to get overwhelmed. Not to be distraught. Not to sneer at others. But simply do our part.

To say "Let go and let God" is to endorse complacency, which has us sitting on the sidelines. If you're a follower of Christ, you're an agent assigned to aid in the healing of your corner of the universe. God is still the God of every situation — but more than that, God is the God *in* the situation, suffering with us, embracing the broken, restoring wounded hearts, and wanting for us to get involved too.

Even you. Even if you have a past, like me. Even if you've been beat down, like me. Even if you feel far, feel lost, feel unworthy. God takes the worst of us, the most shattered and damaged and rebellious and prideful, and reverses our entropy into pulsing life. He sees a desert and says, "I see a garden." God can take a miserable sinner like me and you and breathe something brand new into these jagged veins. This is the work of Christ, shaping us, connecting us, healing us.

I don't believe that every pain has a lesson — but I do believe that every pain can be subverted. I believe that *when I am weak, then I am strong.*[79] I believe He can work through every sin and every ounce of suffering for a far greater tapestry than my own: one that is filled with beggars, the blind, the lame, prostitutes, aristocrats, lepers, demoniacs, murderers, and snot-nosed tax collectors.

Yes, even you and me.

I choose to believe, with my weak little faith, that the righteousness and restoration we need comes from Jesus. It's out of his own self-initiated, one-way, just-because love, which expects nothing back, that our hearts could be big enough to do the same. I believe, in the end, that the cross cuts us down to our true size and exposes our great need. But there in the cross, we also have a Great Savior, who does not say, *"Look what you did to me,"* but instead, *"Look what I've done for you."* This is the only kind of grace that will wreck my sin and bring me back to who I was meant to be. It is the only kind of grace that can put together a dying world.

I hold onto this hope. It's not easy. It's not simple. It's not my immediate instinct. It feels foolish some days: but on those days, it's all I have.

Most days — I trust He is all I need.

"For Christianity is a fighting religion. It thinks God has made the world ... But it also thinks that a great many things have gone wrong with the world that God made and that God insists, and insists very loudly, on our putting them right again."[80]
— C.S. Lewis

---

[79] 2 Corinthians 12:10
[80] C.S. Lewis, *Mere Christianity* (NY: HarperCollins, 1952, 1980) p. 38

When I go to the bookstore, I'll grab books and read the last few pages. I want to know how it ends. I want to know where we end up. Hollywood executives always read the first and last page of a screenplay, and if the characters don't change, they toss the script. We inherently want a landing, a safe conclusion, a final punctuation on the sentence of life.

When I first read the Bible for myself, I started at Revelation. I wanted to know if everything was going to be okay. I heard about the Fall of Man and all the ugly things that happened in Genesis; I knew about the flood and the tower of Babel and the incest and the wars. In Revelation, I was overwhelmed. Everything was getting put right again. Justice was unrolling from Heaven, angels speaking with mere men, evil squashed to pieces, healing was all over the place. Since then, I read the Bible very differently. I know that the first page doesn't get to say everything about us, and we get a landing, a final sentence of victory. We get to win, because God does.

—J.S.

RESOLVING THE UNRESOLVED TENSION:
The vanquishing of evil

[CHAPTER 7]

Chapter 7

Resolving The Unresolved Tension: The Vanquishing of Evil

"The world may be broken, but hope is not crazy."
— John Green[81]

Why God?

If you're like me, you're still skeptical.

There's still unresolved tension.

I still ask:

If God is real — Why did He geopolitically confine Himself to one people-group and one nation on the entire earth? Why didn't He equally manifest Himself to other people-groups? Did everyone else in China and Australia and Africa and the other unknown continents simply go to Hell?

If God is real — Why does He allow certain kinds of suffering? I understand that suffering is part of the human condition. What I don't understand is the *degree* and *extent* to which it occurs almost at random. Why did my cousin Jimmy have to be born brain-dead and suffer for twelve years in a crib before dying a miserable death without even knowing who he was? How is this part of God's plan?

---

[81] https://www.youtube.com/watch?v=qp5P-8adG4w

If God is real — Why do billions of Christians have so many conflicts and contradictions and animosity within the "church"? How could so many people have it wrong, and how could so many of us think "I have it right"? There are so many "Christians" who hardly fit the definition of a sane human being.

If God is real — Why don't more miracles happen on a regular basis? I don't mean all the time, or even frequently. If I were God, I would probably answer a couple more prayers on sickness and disasters, or at least make a *very* visible miracle once in a while that would defy physics and cause the media to say, "Well that was God."

If God is real — Why would I even want to go to Heaven? I understand about not going to Hell, but going to Heaven means I would *lose all the hurts that made me who I am,* and effectively extract the part of my soul that was formed over a lifetime of trials and lessons. Heaven, a place of pure unmitigated happiness, would essentially steal my identity.

I could go on.

But one of the reasons I even came to Christ was because all my questions pointed to a bigger one.

Why do I even ask these questions at all?

Why do I even have this sense of "unresolved tension"?

When I ask, "Why God?" — why even ask why?

Why did the world bother me so much?

A part of me saw a crooked line instead of a straight one, and I wondered how I came to this reality of "crooked." I needed a correction of the universe, some kind of proper justice, a sort of setting-right of the world. How could we know things are very wrong *unless* there must be a very right? Why do we feel anguish at injustice unless we knew of justice?

I'm sure a philosopher or psychologist or very witty blogger could beat me here point-by-point. I've heard them all, and frankly, I'm jaded by all the debating.

In the end, my understanding of reality without God was very grim, and if *all* of us were crying out for a type of healing to take place — could this point to an even greater hope? Could it point to some cosmic answer?

The Gospel — the Good News of Jesus — presented a compelling case.

1) God wrote Himself into the story of broken humanity to bring about healing, and

2) He began the process of this healing by creating a reversal of normal human order at one point in time, in one place, effective for all eternity.

So I had a choice now. I could choose to believe this never happened, and when I die, I die. Annihilation. That's all, folks.

Or I could choose to believe that there is Good News, and at some point in history, God came down and infused the world with His goodness, and that **He alone was the final answer to this *tension of an unresolved humanity*.** His incarnation answered these gut-wrenching questions about life, theology, humanity, and most of all, suffering.

But more than the incarnation of Jesus, I was struck by the Resurrection. This was not just another teaching, but a *historical event,* and it was not going away.

Even if nothing in the Christian faith made sense, at the very least, I would have to explain a ridiculous event two-thousand years ago that made the Jews just go nuts. I would have to accommodate for a cataclysmic shift in the Roman Empire. I would have to come up with some other workable theory about why the Jewish people, who were hell-bent against idols for thousands of years, would suddenly change their Temple services to Sunday mornings and martyr themselves for the Christian faith. I could go on here, too. The evidence is overwhelmingly sufficient that something crazy happened there — as if maybe someone got up from the dead.

Some days, I think this is all just utterly impossible. I feel my faith slipping out sideways, spilling, seeping, oozing, just a puddle of church experiences on the floor.

But when I stack the evidence from both sides against each other, it's just about even. Every side makes sense, and if they wanted to, they could argue from the opposing position. I could persuade you that there's no God just as quickly as I could compel you that there might be one. There are prepackaged syllogisms and pre-defended arguments that have run the same circuits, ad nauseam. It turns out that I like both sides and that both sides even like each other.[82] They're often misinformed and biased, but they're also witty, eloquent, and winsome. You could keep them at checkmate forever.

So I have to choose.

Each day, almost kicking and screaming, I choose to believe the Gospel. Each day, *it is still a tough choice.* I have seen and done some horrible things. I have every reason to continue doubting God. I still have hard questions. But while I daily wrestle with doubts, I still choose to believe.

---

[82] In the round of debates between the late Christopher Hitchens and Douglas Wilson, you can see they're practically friends.

Most days, there is just a tiny mustard seed of faith that beats this struggling heart — and most days, it is enough.

Please understand that I'm not saying this is acceptable for every Christian. God does want us to have a robust, vibrant, thriving faith. I am not at all giving permission to just have the bare minimum. But this is God's grace: that we all get in by *faith*. I spent years measuring myself to on-fire believers, and I'm simply just not one of them. My faith burns slower, more methodical, seated in the back, plagued with questions, desperate in prayer, trusting those rare moments when Christ is fully visible.

I do want all my questions answered: but what I care about is what makes me *whole*. The Gospel had this for me. It plugged in all the missing pieces.

It was also intellectually satisfying. I did my homework, too. I started to see that the Bible describes the human condition all too well. Things in reality line up with Scripture. The history is sound. I've seen too many supernatural occurrences to be so easily explained. I've seen the Spirit of God do incredible work in peoples' lives. The transformation is not natural. Maybe that sounds silly to you, but again: you can choose to believe that, or not.

It turns out I'm not alone in this. Many Christians struggle to believe, but they keep serving anyway. They get by on their weak little faith. They are not intimidated by doubts, and though they often walk through a fog of their own questions, they continue pursuing Christ. They do not cower from these needles of mystery, but recognize it is a part of their spiritual journey, and that it really is okay to wonder sometimes.

"I have learned to live with the rise and fall of the thoughts and feelings of faith, I co-exist with honest doubt, to accept tension and paradox without clinging to it as an excuse for inaction ... I am trying to do what people of faith have always done — respond to revelation by my own best lights, struggle to understand all that can be understood and have reverence for the rest, act beyond my certain knowledge in the faith that such action is blessed."[83]

— Daniel Taylor

"The faith that can't be shaken is the faith that has been shaken."[84]

— Randy Alcorn

"When things go wrong, you ask yourself, 'How can there be a good God?' I think the conclusion that I come to, is that both faith and doubt are equally logical choices in the face of tragedy. Faith is to say, 'Yes, a future will have pain,' but there is a meaning and a purpose deeper than that pain. For me, that is my choice, to believe *rather than doubt."[85]*

— Jon Foreman

"Trust in the LORD with all your heart
and lean not on your own understanding;
in all your ways acknowledge him,
and he will make your paths straight."

— Proverbs 3:5-6

---

[83] Daniel Taylor, *The Myth of Certainty* (IL: InterVarsity Press, 1986, 1992) p. 145

[84] Randy Alcorn, *If God Is Good* (CO: Multnomah, 2009) p. 4

[85] http://refreshedmag.com/switchfoot-balancing-faith-families-music-and-the-love-of-surfing/

Friday / Saturday / Sunday

I think no one else was more swamped by doubts than the disciples.

What I mean is, Jesus's disciples didn't know he would come back to life. That Friday, they only saw the horror of the cross. They didn't know that the forces of evil would be subverted toward victory: that even the death of Jesus was working towards a greater glory.

At this moment, we live between the Cross and the Resurrection.

We live inside Saturday.

We are waiting for Sunday.

Sometimes there's unresolved tension, and we need to let it bleed. Pain can be pain and nothing more. I don't expect it all to work out. That's life.

But occasionally, we get glimpses of Sunday. We get an infinitesimal glance into what God is really doing. We see how something connected, the barest sketch of His infinite mind.

The biggest glance, perhaps, is the day Jesus rose.

Jesus dying on a cross showed an unresolved tension that bled — but Jesus out of a tomb showed there really is a bow-tie to this whole thing, a far-off nearly imperceptible light at the end of this tunnel. It means we are not at the end of the story. We have a hope that God is somehow working all things for an eternal good, displaying his limitless love on a cross, compensating for all the pain in human history within the most horrific tragedy of all.

When I see the cross, it's possible that *God could use what He hates to achieve what He loves.* It's possible He must make impossible decisions in a vastly disarrayed universe for a greater, glorious end. Maybe we'll find out the "reasons" one day for why everything happened. Maybe they will satisfy us, or not. But by then, the answers probably won't matter. We'll be face to face with the God who was with us all along, the only one who never left us in our hurt, the one who has truly conquered the dragon.

For now, we live in the tension. We ride out Saturday.

I won't always like it. I won't always get it. I don't know why He makes the choices He does. But I want to trust that He knows what He's doing. I want to trust that in a sin-torn world, He is making the best possible choices — and that our pain breaks His heart.

Maybe it did. Maybe those three days were an overarching reflection of the human cosmos, and we are waiting for the threads to pull together. Maybe at the end, we will find a love stronger than death, and we're invited in today.

Friday is the wound.

Saturday is the suffering.

But Sunday — glorious Sunday.

I wait. I press on.

V.18 — *For I consider that our present sufferings are not worth comparing with the glory that will be revealed in us.*

V. 28 — *And we know that in all things God works for the good of those who love him, who have been called according to his purpose.*

V. 31 — *What, then, shall we say in response to this? If God is for us, who can be against us?*

— Romans 8

You intended to harm me, but God intended it for good
to accomplish what is now being done, the saving of many lives.
— Genesis 50:20

"I have told you these things,
so that in me you may have peace.
In this world you will have trouble.
But take heart! I have overcome the world."
— John 16:33, the words of Jesus

See You Again:
This Is Not The End, My Friend

"Hope is a memory of the future."[86]
— Gabriel Marcel

The Resurrection of Jesus tells me this world is not our final home.

Over twelve years ago, I went to a funeral for my friend. He was eighteen years old. He was stabbed to death in the doorway of his home, and he had died trying to save his sister and his mother. He died on the way to the hospital. When I got the news, I hung up the phone and threw it across the room. I kicked over a chair and couldn't stop yelling.

---

[86] A paraphrase from Gabriel Marcel, *Homo Viator: Introduction to a Metaphysic of Hope* (Chicago: Henry Regnery, 1951) p. 53

At the funeral, there he was. An eighteen year old life, cut short, dreams gone, a future inside a box.

Three months before he died, he and I were at a Christian retreat together. During one of the services, he received Jesus Christ as Lord and Savior. I was there when it happened.

At the funeral — we were able to rejoice. It was not an easy rejoicing. But we knew he was with Jesus, in a joyous union that we could hardly comprehend. He's there now, and ten years has probably felt like ten seconds.

I don't mean to make this a cheerful story. That would be impossible. It's just that it's difficult to connect the Resurrection to our daily lives: until you're at a funeral. Then it makes sense.

I'm not saying his death makes sense, or that it doesn't hurt, or that I fully accept what God is doing all the time. I'm saying: the Resurrection gives a hope above and beyond all that happens. It answers our deepest fears about eternity. If Jesus is alive, then a funeral is not really a funeral — and futures do not stop in a box.

The death of death is the Great Reversal of the human story. Even those who overcome many obstacles have to die one day. Jesus reversed inevitability. He is the True Story of the world. He made it okay to dream again, even when dreams seem to die. In the midst of cynicism, Jesus is the "happily ever after" we all secretly long for.

Jesus is the hope in traffic, in troubled family, in bad grades, in aging, in failed plans, in irreversible mistakes, in overwhelming bills, in second and third chances, in tragic headlines, in our daily struggle. In the shadow of death, his shadow is greater still.

Sean: I'll see you again soon one day.

Until then: we tell the story.

Dear cousin Jimmy,

You died about fifteen years ago. When I met you, you were screaming in pain but you didn't know why. You were born almost completely brain-dead; you could only eat, drink, breathe, scream, laugh, and cry. I had the honor of making you laugh once by making a funny face. Or maybe you just laughed at my face.

Your parents loved you to death. Your dad even risked jail time like that movie John Q. to get you medical care. You know all that now. He tried but he couldn't save you. He loved you more than I have ever seen a human being love anyone.

I know you're in Heaven right now because God protects His children. You didn't need to be saved: you were safe. People might have questioned why God made you that way, but now you're beautiful. You can run, think, draw, jump, build, point, sing, shout, tumble, bounce, dance, rock, roll, and eat by yourself. You can lift more weights, sing higher notes, and write better songs than I ever could. You're with Jesus, and probably both of you are laughing at my face.

It must have been exciting to hear for the first time what Jesus did for you. You got to hear it straight from his mouth. I'm trying not to weep thinking about how wonderful it is where you are. By the grace of God I'll see you again real soon, Jimmy. I might even have a fighting chance of writing some better songs than you.

—J.S.

"May God bless you with discomfort at easy answers, half truths, and superficial relationships, so that you may live deep within your heart.

"May God bless you with anger at injustice, oppression, and exploitation of people, so that you may work for justice, freedom and peace.

"May God bless you with tears to shed for those who suffer from pain, rejection, starvation, and war, so that you may reach out your hand to comfort them and to turn their pain in to joy.

"And may God bless you with enough foolishness to believe that you can make a difference in this world, so that you can do what others claim cannot be done. To bring justice and kindness to all our children and the poor.

"Amen."

— Franciscan Benediction

When I ask if God is good
I see a cross, an empty tomb.
What He writ large in the stars
is writ small for our wounds.
From the sky to my sin
He is re-making us again.
When nothing else is good,
He is the only one who is.
—J.S.

UPSIDE-DOWN VALLEY:

Where the mountain touches the sky and heaven breaks open

[CONCLUSION]

Conclusion
Upside-Down Valley:
Where The Mountain Touches The Sky and Heaven Breaks Open

I can't imagine how difficult it must be to have leprosy.

It was even worse in the first century.

You can't shop for groceries. You can't go to school or to church or get a job. You're never allowed to marry or to have children. No one wants to be friends with you, much less come near you. If someone approaches you on the street or walks past your doorway, you have to yell out, "I'm unclean." You're most definitely a beggar or living off family wealth.

If you had leprosy: you are untouchable, from your skin to your heart.

One day, you hear about a prophet who talks about the *Kingdom of God.* His name is John. He eats grasshoppers and wears camels and cows. He's baptizing people in the water, actually *purifying* them in the Jordan. He keeps talking about someone greater who is coming, another Prophet whose feet were too worthy to touch.

You're a leper. You have a lot of time. You make the entire day's trip into town to get to the Jordan. The whole way, you're yelling, "Unclean, unclean, unclean." You lose a finger. A toenail falls off. You arrive at the Jordan at night, the stars heavy and the clouds just whispers. You hear the murmurs of hundreds, no, *thousands* of people in line by the side of the river. The moon is fragmented upon the surface, a wrinkled blue globe that has lit the faces of the weary.

Almost the moment you get there, a man in torn clothes says, "Behold! The Lamb of God who has come to take away the sins of the world!"

At first you think he's talking about you, and your stomach turns inside-out. But you can *feel* someone just past your shoulder, the crowds parting for him. You're used to this; the crowds have parted for you, too. Crowds have hissed at you, booed you, blamed you for your disease, said that you were cursed, blamed your parents and your ancestors and your lack of faith. Just seeing the lines of people move back puts a dull echo in your chest. Your illness touches every part of your life.

You see the man, this supposed Lamb of God. He walks through the split sea of people and enters the water. The man in torn clothes, John, is shaking. He is near hysterical. John blurts out, "You must baptize me." The Lamb-Man says, "No, John. You must baptize me. To fulfill all righteousness." For a moment, they have their hands on each other's shoulders. Everyone is fidgeting, frozen, waiting for their turn.

John dunks the Lamb in the water.

Then it happens.

You look up, and the moon twists in half. The stars scatter in every direction. The darkness swirls in blue and purple. You feel the river and the air reversing outward. A wind pushes through the Jordan and the water peels away and the people raise their arms gasping.

You haven't smelled a thing in years, but you catch the faintest hint of salt. You close your eyes for a moment, remembering. You are back there, with your mother, near the water when your hands could still build sandcastles. You are there, before your body began to waste away, piece by terrible piece, before this sickness stole you. You are there, your father raising you to the sun, above mountains and towards heaven, flying up and up to worlds unknown, when anything was possible.

Those dreams are just dreams. Gone, dust. But you remember.

You hear a low roar, louder and louder. Then the sky expands, breaks open, dances in circles, and a soft pouring light washes over John and the Lamb. The light is pulsing, like the wings of a bird suspended in time.

You hear a voice.

"You are my Son. It's you I love. With you, I am well pleased."

You're certain this voice is for the man who's being baptized. But you suspect that it could be for you, too.

The sky closes. The stars return. The wind dials down and the river is still. The moon is whole in the water again.

You look for the Lamb-Man, but he's gone. There's a sudden swell of conversation, but the line resumes and John continues to baptize.

You leave. You need to find this Lamb. You slink back through the streets, through the dark, saying "Unclean" without thinking, looking for this man. You know his face. You saw every detail under that glowing beam of heaven.

Over a month passes. You've been looking for him every day. There are rumors he has taken pilgrimage to the desert, which could mean he has died. Some say he went to fight the devil; others say he went to atone for his sin. You know plenty of sinners, but none of them could break the sky in half.

Then you hear the Lamb-Man is in town. You hear that he's been *healing diseases.* They say that about a lot of prophets. Anyone could be a messiah these days: just say you healed someone who was already getting better, and you're suddenly the Voice of God. You're skeptical. He could be another charlatan, a hustler, a fake.

It's not hard to find him. Everyone else in town is scrambling after him. You hear others saying, "Yeshua is here. The King. The Messiah."

You press through the people, yelling, "Unclean, unclean." The townspeople move back. As you get closer to the man they call Yeshua, you notice a small circle of men and women around him, but they're not moving away. They don't make a face at you. One of them even steps toward you.

You fall to your knees in front of Yeshua with your head bowed. You'll probably lose a toe. But with these prophets, you have to make a big show of everything.

You say, "If you are willing, you can make me clean."

Then you're jolted. You look up. The man Yeshua has actually *touched your shoulder.*

You look into his face. He is just a man. He is near tears.

He says to you, "I am willing. Be clean."

Another jolt, but this time it goes through your body. You look first at your hands. Your *hands.* You have all your fingers. You pull back your sleeves and your skin, your *skin,* you can feel your skin again. You touch your face and it's whole, it's there, everything is there.

Yeshua brings you to your feet. He says, "Please do not tell this to anyone. Show yourself to the priest and offer the sacrifices that Moses commanded for your cleansing, as a testimony."

And he hugs you. He kisses you on both cheeks. Your knees nearly buckle.

You are healed.

Of course, you have to tell everyone. You run through town, yelling, "Clean, clean!" You run to your family, to the market, to the church, running and running. "I'm clean! Yeshua has healed me!"

Soon you discover that the townspeople are rushing after the Lamb of God, taking to the streets in droves, looking for him. Yeshua and his circle of followers cannot stay; the crowds have grown too thick. They head to the next town.

You head back into town, to be restored again to the people.

A few years later, you hear they've accused this man of blasphemy, of claiming to be God, of revolting against Rome. He is sentenced to death.

You make the journey to Jerusalem. You love running now. You run to the Prefect's courtyards, the public square for judicial hearings. You hear that Pontius Pilate, the current Prefect of Rome, has ordered Yeshua to be flogged. It's the very worst sort of punishment that leaves a man in tattered bloody shreds. Somehow, Yeshua has survived the torture.

In the courtyard, dozens of people are shouting for crucifixion.

You're confused. This is the man who has healed hundreds of people. He tore open the sky. He taught the ancient words of Scripture. Even if he had been revolting against Rome, a crucifixion was an unspoken curse among men; it would mean you are completely untouchable, both here and in the afterlife.

Two Roman guards drag out Yeshua from behind the pillars of the court. He looks even worse than you imagined. His skin is hanging in flaps. Blood is still gushing from his body, his head, his chest. Some of his teeth are gone.

You remember this. When your teeth began to fall out. When your skin would flake and tear away.

You want to speak out against his murder: but the crowd is overpowering. You might be accused of being an accomplice. So you stay silent.

Pontius Pilate, dressed in the most ornate silver armor and purple robes, hushes the people. He says, "I have here two criminals." A second man is dragged out from behind the pillars, a man in chains. Pilate continues, "This man is the rabble-rouser Barabbas. He has killed Roman citizens and several of the Jewish family. This other man is Yeshua the prophet. He has done no harm that I can see. As customary to the Passover, I shall release one man back to you as amnesty for his sin. You may choose the man."

The people, without pausing, yell, "Barabbas."

You can hardly believe it. Pilate flinches and the guards are uncertain. In slow steps, they whisk Yeshua away, behind the pillars, to his death.

Barabbas is free. Yeshua is condemned.

You suddenly remember something. About the day Yeshua healed you.

He had asked you to re-instate your citizenship with the priest, so that you may be part of the community again. He had asked you not to tell anyone about the healing, but you did. From that day forth, Yeshua could not return to the town, but stayed on the fringes in solitary places.

I was able to walk freely in the town, but Yeshua was not.

He and I had switched places.

You are jolted again.

I am Barabbas. I am the sinner set free. I am Pilate, who turned a blind eye to glory.

You want to stop this madness, but they have taken Yeshua outside the city with a cross on his back, all the way to Golgotha, the Edge of the Skull. It is the hill of the damned.

You follow. You are familiar with slinking to the edge of the walls.

He is there. He is raised. He shouts. He is crucified.

You are seeing yourself, a twisted, mangled body, untouchable and unclean.

I am Barabbas. I am Pilate. I am the leper, made clean.

Yeshua is buried. The day is gone, and then another. It is quiet; the town has hushed. The disciples have ran, and you have forgotten the name of the crucified man.

But Sunday morning, you hear a small stirring.

There is a rumor.

There is a rumor that he is alive.

There is a rumor that Yeshua has appeared to many, with scars in his hands and feet, with a scar in the side of his heart. He has appeared even to his disciples, the ones who abandoned him, to restore them to God once again.

It would mean this healing is more than my body.
It would mean I can be healed for eternity.
You wonder if you should see.
You wonder.
It is just a rumor.
But oh, if the rumor was true.
If only it could be true.

— J.S.

Acknowledgements

A huge thank you to every single test-reader. You caught typos, cheered me on, offered tough critiques, and invested your time into making this book better than I could ever do on my own.

Thank you to my wonderful friends who gave me permission to write about their stories.

Thank you to the awesome communities of Tumblr and Wordpress, who have stretched me and challenged me to really meet people where they are.

Thank you to Paul Kim, Jake English, Calvin Kim, Hoon Park, T.B. LaBerge, Lauren Britt, Jerry Edmonds, Danny Esposito, Jacob Choe, Alex Choe, Christina Choe, Grace Choe, Austin Cho, Andre Holmes, Teena Oh, Tim Ryu, Susan Chung, Christine Ko, Rob Connelly, and Jerry Em. Each of you were there during a difficult season of life and gave me the grace and wisdom to endure.

Thank you again to Rob Connelly for the cover and Crae Achacoso for the artwork.

Of course, to my amazing wife, who forfeited sleep to listen to me read from this book, and encouraged me the entire way. You are my best friend and I'm excited for our continued journey of marriage, to the horizon together.

To Yeshi: savior, friend, Lord, King.

If you've been blessed by this book,
please consider leaving a review on Amazon!
Other titles available by J.S. Park —

What The Church Won't Talk About

All the tough questions we've wanted to ask in church, from sex to doubt to politics to conflict to depression, in a collection of the most viral Q&As from J.S. Park's blog. For both the absolute skeptic and the veteran Christian, with real stories from real people.

The Christianese Dating Culture

Is there any real wisdom the church can offer for those who are dating, single, wounded, or think "it's too late for me?" Sifting through Josh Harris, Taylor Swift, romantic comedies, and the heart of Jesus, we find relevant truth and hopeful grace for relationships.

Cutting It Off

Porn addiction is real and it nearly ruined my life. I was a porn addict for fifteen years, and I've now been sober for over three. I want to offer you recovery, not just for weeks at a time, but quitting for good.

23382795R00136

Made in the USA
Middletown, DE
23 August 2015